**Also by Peter Handke**

# The Ride Across
# Lake Constance
## AND OTHER PLAYS

# PETER HANDKE

# *The Ride Across Lake Constance*

## AND OTHER PLAYS

*Translated by* MICHAEL ROLOFF
*in collaboration with Karl Weber*

**FARRAR, STRAUS AND GIROUX** / NEW YORK

# Contents

*Prophecy*

*Where to begin?*
*Everything is out of joint and totters.*
*The air quivers with comparisons.*
*No word is better than the other,*
*the earth booms with metaphors . . .*
—OSIP MANDELSTAM


*Four speakers* (A, B, C, D)


A
The flies will die like flies.


B
The ruttish dogs will snuffle like ruttish dogs.


C
The pig on the spit will scream like a pig on the spit.


D
The bull will roar like a bull.

A

The statue will stand like a statue.

B

The chickens will scurry like chickens.

C

The madman will run like a madman.

D

The lunatic will howl like a lunatic.

A

The mangy dog will roam like a mangy dog.

B

The vulture will circle like a vulture.

C

The aspen leaves will quiver like aspen leaves.

D

The grass will quiver like grass.

AB

The house of cards will tumble like a house of cards.

AC

The bombs will strike like bombs.

AD

The ripe fruit will fall from the trees like ripe fruit.

BC
The water on the hot stone will hiss like water on a hot stone.

BD
Those who are doomed to die will stand like those who are doomed to die.

ABCD
The stuck pig will bleed like a stuck pig.

A
The average person will behave like an average person.

B
The bastard will behave like a bastard.

C
The man of honor will behave like a man of honor.

D
The opera hero will behave like an opera hero.

A
The stepchild will be treated like a stepchild.
The miracle worker will be awaited like a miracle worker.
The freak will be stared at like a freak.
The Messiah will be longed for like the Messiah.
The milch cow will be exploited like a milch cow.
The lepers will be shunned like lepers.
Hell will be hated like hell.
The shroud will be spread out like a shroud.
The mad dog will be shot like a mad dog.

B
The fool will prattle like a fool.
The parrot will prattle like a parrot.

The roaches will scurry from the light like roaches.
The snow in May will vanish like the snow in May.
The child will be happy like a child.
The miracle will happen like a miracle.
The corpse in the pool will swell up like a corpse in a pool.
The thunderclap will be like a thunderclap.

CD
The trooper will swear like a trooper.
The frog will leap like a frog.
Lightning will flash like lightning.
The thief will sneak off like a thief.
The horse will eat like a horse.
The school child will hide like a school child.
The splash in the water will be like a splash in the water.
The slap in the face will be like a slap in the face.
The viper will strike like a viper.

BCD
The wounded horses will rear up like wounded horses.
The jockey will be alert like a jockey.
The huskies will howl like huskies.
The Jew will haggle like a Jew.
The fish will wriggle on the hook like a fish on a hook.
The open wound will fester like an open wound.
The virgin will put on airs like a virgin.
The choirboy will walk like a choirboy.
The sailor will walk like a sailor.
The Spaniard will walk like a Spaniard.
Gary Cooper will walk like Gary Cooper.
Donald Duck will walk like Donald Duck.

A
The wet poodle will stand there like a wet poodle.
The poor sinner will stand there like a poor sinner.

The cow will stand before the new barn door like a cow before a new barn door.
The rooster on the dungheap will stand like a rooster on a
dungheap.

AB

The felled tree will crash like a felled tree.
The maniac will fight like a maniac.
The cat will slink around the hot soup like a cat around
hot soup.
The dogs will hide from the thunderstorm like dogs hiding
from a thunderstorm.
The roaring lion will stalk about like a roaring lion.
The wildfire will spread like wildfire.

ABC

The hyenas will howl like hyenas.
The nightwatchman will yawn like a nightwatchman.
The conspirators will whisper like conspirators.
The reeds in the wind will rustle like reeds in the wind.
The ostrich will bury its head in the sand like an ostrich.
The grass widow will tremble like a grass widow.
The rat will sleep like a rat.
The dog will die like a dog.

ABCD

The shoe will fit like a shoe on a foot.

A

The plague will spread like the plague.

B

The rose will smell like a rose.

C

The swarm of bees will buzz like a swarm of bees.

D

Your shadow will follow you like a shadow.

A

The tomb will be silent like a tomb.
The monument will stand like a monument.

B

A man will rise up like a man.
The cliff will stand in the surf like a cliff in the surf.

C

The cloudburst will approach like a cloudburst.
The ants will bite like ants.

D

The tidal wave will swell like a tidal wave.
The flock of frightened sheep will scatter like a flock of
frightened sheep.

A

The sand will run through your fingers like sand.

B

In the theater you will feel like a theatergoer.

C

One egg will resemble another as one egg another.

ABC

A scream will issue from the mouth of the crowd as out of
one mouth.

D

The organ pipes will stand like organ pipes.
The trumpets of the Last Judgment will ring out like the
trumpets of the Last Judgment.
The revelation will be like a revelation.

C

The mole will tunnel through the lawn like a mole.

B

The voice from another world will sound like a voice from
another world.

A

The avalanche will hurtle like an avalanche.
Those who have lost their senses will behave like people who
have lost their senses.

AB

The prophet will make faces like a prophet.
The angels will speak as with angels' tongues.
The moth will flutter to the light like a moth to the light.
The barn door will be open like a barn door.

ABC

The scales will fall from your eyes like scales falling from
your eyes.
The foreign body will be spewed out like a foreign body.
The rats will leave the sinking ship like rats leaving a sinking
ship.
God will step before mankind like God.

AB

The bear will sleep like a bear.

A
The wall will stand like a wall.

D
The cornfield will rustle like a cornfield.

DC
After the rain the mushrooms will mushroom like mushrooms
after the rain.

DCB
The nutshell will rock on the water like a nutshell on the
water.

DCBA
The migratory birds will flock like migratory birds.
Those who walk on a cloud will walk as if on a cloud.
Those who are struck by thunder will be like thunderstruck
people.
Those who are in seventh heaven will feel as if they were in
seventh heaven.
Those stung by a scorpion will leap up like those who are
stung by a scorpion.

AD
Ebb and flood will alternate like ebb and flood.
The fish in the water will flit about like fish in the water.
Water and fire will be compatible like water and fire.
Day and night will be as different as day and night.

B
You will live in clover like someone living in clover.

C
The dream will seem to you like a dream.

B
Eternity will seem to you like an eternity.

ABCD
But the fish in the sea shall be plentiful like fish in the sea.
But the sand at the shore shall be plentiful like sand at the
shore.
But the stars in the heavens shall be plentiful like stars in the
heavens.
But the people on earth shall be plentiful like people on
earth.

A
And the rabbits will multiply like rabbits.

B
And the germs will multiply like germs.

C
And the poor will multiply like the poor.

D
And a man like you and me will be a man like you and me.

A
Daily bread will be needed like daily bread.

B
Blood will be red like blood.

C
The wind will be swift like wind.

D
Poison will be yellow like poison.

A

Molasses will be sticky like molasses.

B

The fool will be gentle like a fool.

C

Life will be complex like life.

D

The sieve will be holey like a sieve.

A

The ultimate things will be unutterable like ultimate things.

B

The razor's edge will be sharp like a razor's edge.

C

The universe will be infinite like a universe.

D

The picky eater will be skinny like a picky eater.

A

The barrel will be round like a barrel.

B

The nigger will be uppity like a nigger.

C

The father will be to the son as father to son.

D

The ride in the jalopy will be bumpy like a ride in a jalopy.

A
The Pope will be infallible like the Pope.

B
The novel will be fantastic like a novel.

C
The movie will be unreal like a movie.

D
The needle in the haystack will be hard to find like a needle
in a haystack.

A
The night will be silent like the night.

B
Sin will be black like sin.

C
The soul will be inexhaustible like the soul.

D
The well will be deep like a well.

A
The sponge will be wet like a sponge.

B
The poet will be dreamy like a poet.

C
The others will be entirely like the others.

D

Death will be inevitable like death.

A

The morrow will be inevitable like the morrow.

B

The amen in the prayer will be inevitable like the amen in
the prayer.

C

Something will be as inevitable as only something can be
inevitable.

D

The peacock will be proud like a peacock.

ABCD

And the transformed will feel like those transformed.

And those who are turned into pillars of salt will stand there
like ones turned into pillars of salt.

And those who are struck by lightning will fall like ones
struck by lightning.

And the spellbound will listen like spellbound people.

And the paralyzed will stand like paralyzed people.

And the beckoned will come like beckoned people.

And the lame will stand like lame people.

And those struck by thunder will stand there like thunderstruck people.

And the sleeping will walk like sleepwalkers.

And those who have been called but not chosen will stand
there like ones called but not chosen.

And the substitutes will feel like substitutes.

And the people by the mirror will look at themselves like
people in front of the mirror.

And the newborn will feel like the newborn.

And the beaten will feel like beaten people.
And those who have been swallowed up by the earth will be
 like ones swallowed up by the earth.

**A**
The reality will become reality.

**B**
The truth will become truth.

**AB**
The ice will freeze like ice.

**ABC**
The ends will stand on end.

**ABCD**
The bottom will plunge to the bottom.

**ABC**
Nothingness will become nothing.

**AB**
The ashes will turn to ashes.

**B**
The air will turn to air.

**A**
The dust will turn to dust.

**D**
The weasel will be weasel-faced.

**C**
The feather will be feather-light.

B
Acid will be acid-fast.

A
Chalk will be chalk-white.

D
Butter will be butter-soft.

C
Lightning will be lightning-fast.

B
The hair will be a hairsbreadth thin.

A
Death will be deadly dull.

D
The dead will be deathly pale.

C
The dying will feel deathly ill.

B
Pitch will be pitch-black.

A
The heart will be heartsick.

D
The skin will be skin-deep.

C
The bloodsucker will be bloodthirsty.

B

The threads will be threadbare.

A

The stone will be stone-hard.

ABCD

Every day will be like every other.

**Translated by Michael Roloff**

*Calling for Help*

although the number of people who may participate in this *Sprechstück* is unlimited, it requires a minimum of two speakers (male or female). the speakers' objective is to show the way to the sought-after word HELP, a way that leads across many sentences and words. the speakers are playing the need for help without, however, being in a situation that really requires help; they are playing the need *acoustically*. while the way to the word help is being demonstrated, the sentences and words are not uttered with their usual meaning, but only to signify that help is being sought. while the speakers are seeking the *word* help they are in need of *help*; once having found the *word* help they no longer need any help. before they find the word they ask *for* help, whereas once they have found the word help they only speak *help* without needing to ask *for* help any longer. once able to shout help, they no longer need to shout *for* help; they are relieved that they can shout help. the word HELP has lost its meaning.

on their way to the word help, the speakers repeatedly approach the proximate meaning or only the acoustic proximity of the sought-after word: the respective NO-response that greets each attempt also changes according to the degree of proximity; the formal tension of the speaking increases; the course that this tension prescribes resembles, say, the rising and falling decibel curve during a soccer match; the closer one team gets to the goal of the other, the more the spectator noise increases, dying off again after each unsuccessful or impeded attempt to score, then swelling again, etc., until the word HELP is found during the final onslaught; then pure joy reigns among the speakers.

the spectators and listeners quickly recognize the speakers' objective. however, should the spectators indicate to the speakers, as spectators are wont to during punch-and-judy shows, that they know what the speakers need, and should they shout HELP, in that event the speakers, like performers who are threatened by the crocodile in a punch-and-judy show, won't understand what the spectators have in mind, but will understand the helpful shouts of HELP only as *genuine* distress calls, which only bother the speakers during their *play*. once the speakers have found the word help, it is repeated as a triumphant shout, so often that its meaning becomes an ovation to the *word* help. when the ovation becomes nearly unbearable, the mass chorus breaks off and a single speaker instantly speaks the word HELP by himself, neither expressing gladness with it nor that he is seeking help. the word HELP is uttered that way once.

the speakers also may drink COCA-COLA at intervals.

and in conclusion, while we think of all of you once more, we call on you and invite you to search with us for ways to mutual understanding, to deepened knowledge, to an open heart, to a fraternal life in the one truly world-embracing community of men: NO.

immediately after the assassination the authorities employed all available means to obtain a clear picture of the murder: NO. don't worry too much but enjoy the good times: NO. the claim that these persons were compelled to enter the plane is made up of thin air: NO. the dangers of missing the boat in one's profession are minimal at present: NO. those who come after you also want to use the towel: NO. the cripple can't be blamed for being a cripple: NO.

someone has escaped from death row: NO. the head of state has placed a wreath in the name of all the people: NO. unemployment has continued to recede: NO. a few cracks have become visible in the ice: NO. the teacher has reprimanded the unruly student: NO. the high pressure system has moved farther east: NO. an old proverb has something to say: NO. the wounded man's condition has changed for the worse recently: NO. the field marshal has led the courageous troops to victory: NO. silverware and plates have been made germfree: NO.

the queen was wearing a new hat: NO. unknown person is accused of having tipped over several gravestones: NO. the actor swooned while onstage: NO. a moist lip was the motive for the murder: NO. the bones were laid to rest in complete silence: NO. workers at that time were living in inhuman conditions: NO. two nations are entering into a nonaggression pact: NO. the newspaper did not appear yesterday: NO. the moon moved between sun and earth precisely according to calculations: NO. the leader went on foot: NO.

the first-class carriages can be found in the forward part of the train: NO. the mushrooms are no longer as poisonous once they have been cooked: NO. the family constitutes the germinal cell of the state: NO. the newspaper will be twice its usual size due to a special occasion: NO. everyone can eat his fill nowadays: NO. the trains go only as far as the border: NO. even the toughest cop goes soft at the sight of the empress: NO. the girl decorates the table with a rose: NO. due to constantly rising wages we find ourselves forced to announce a small price increase: NO. the king remains silent: NO. english is spoken here: NO. the farmer's sister is in the woods: NO. knives forks scissors and matches are not for little children: NO. the bomb comes from the east: NO. what's right must remain right: NO. our rooms are air-conditioned: NO. the father is working in the field: NO. whoever refuses to listen must be made to feel: NO.

the price includes breakfast: NO. you have entered a restricted area: NO. the train will presumably arrive a few minutes late: NO. we thank you for your visit: NO. illegible requests will be denied: NO. enjoyed in moderate quantities, alcohol is not harmful: NO. have you renewed your driver's license: NO. keep back, police regulations: NO. the missing-persons bureau of the red cross is looking for the following missing persons: NO. a high reward has been placed on the culprit's head: NO. the last row must stay empty: NO. everyone is waiting for the game-ending whistle: NO. belated protests won't be accepted: NO. please set the volume so that the noise will be confined to your room: NO. follow me unobtrusively please: NO. we wish you bon voyage: NO. there should be a death penalty for stealing food from little children: NO. show your hands: NO. green is good for your eyes: NO. the monarch is eager for reforms: NO. give me your i.d.: NO. anyone found on the street after dark will be shot: NO.

beyond this point only at your own risk: NO. keep it warm: NO. tear off here: NO. delete what is inapplicable: NO. enter in back: NO. don't eat for two hours: NO. show your tickets automatically: NO. push in the glass: NO. don't disturb: NO. use the service entrance: NO. read the directions: NO. print in capitals: NO. pull in your head: NO. hold children by the hand: NO. keep the receipt: NO. turn the key twice: NO. don't lose your head: NO. stay calm: NO. don't move the accident victim: NO. don't use spit as a spot remover: NO. be ready to show your i.d. cards: NO. go on: NO. don't fold: NO. wipe your shoes: NO. transfer: NO. make room: NO. apply the tourniquet above the wound: NO. buy now: NO. NO. raise your arm: NO. wait for the official signal: NO. close the doors: NO. protect against sunlight: NO.

in the name of the republic: NO. in one part of yesterday's edition: NO. lunch from twelve to two: NO. a six-month guarantee: NO. the first door to the left: NO. danger, construction: NO. know your terror threshold: NO. hats checked free: NO. hunting season closed from march to september: NO. blood group o: NO. trainee wanted: NO. ocean view: NO. sentenced to death in absentia: NO. measurements 38, 24, 34: NO. before the treatment and after the treatment: NO. nonpotable water: NO. all credit cards accepted: NO. police checkpoint within five thousand yards: NO. because of unprecedented demand: NO. not on saturdays: NO. an unknown victim: NO. next teller please: NO. two to three teaspoonfuls a day: NO. danger: NO. no dining car: NO. from our catalogue: NO. the fifty-second week!: NO. wet paint: NO. open all day today: NO. no cartoons due to the unusual length of the feature: NO. extra: NO. moved, address unknown: NO. only on weekdays: NO. against asthma attacks: NO. platform one: NO. addressee unknown: NO. one-way street: NO. insect repellent: NO. no more war: NO. reserved for women and children: NO. in the tenth round: NO. volunteers step forward: NO. in case of emergency: NO. to the turnpike: NO. towelettes twenty-five cents: NO. this establishment is being struck: NO. freedom for: NO. the penalty is increased by one sleepless night a month plus solitary confinement in complete darkness on the anniversary of the crime: NO.

lights out!: NO. enter!: NO. softly!: NO. thanks!: NO. present!: NO. heads up!: NO. to everyone!: NO. first name!: NO. beginning today!: NO. next!: NO. watch out!: NO. after, you, please!:

NO. profession!: NO. never!: NO. unfortunately!: NO. to the showers!: NO. wanted!: NO. until further notice!: NO. by the neck!: NO. hand it over!: NO. shut the door!: NO. undress!: NO. as of now!: NO. down!: NO. go on!: NO. sit!: NO. back!: NO. inri!: NO. bravo!: NO. hands up!: NO. eyes closed!: NO. smoke!: NO. into the corner!: NO. psst!: NO. aha!: NO. lie!: NO. hands on the table!: NO. up against the wall!: NO. no ifs, ands or buts!: NO. neither forward nor backward!: NO. yes!: NO. no delay!: NO. stretch out!: NO. no stopping!: NO. stop!: NO. fire!: NO. I'm drowning!: NO. ah!: NO. ouch!: NO. no!: NO. hello!: NO. holy!: NO. holy holy holy!: NO. over here!: NO. shut up!: NO. hot!: NO. air!: NO. hiss!: NO. water!: NO. away!: NO. emergency!: NO. never again!: NO. mortal danger!: NO. alarm!: NO. red!: NO. heil!: NO. light!: NO. behind!: NO. don't!: NO. there!: NO. here!: NO. upstairs!: NO. go!: NO. NO. NO:
help?: YES!
help?: YES!
help?: YES!

helYESpYEshelYESpYEshelYESpYEshelYESpYEshelYESpYEshelp

help

**Translated by Michael Roloff**

# *My Foot My Tutor*

*What, I say, my foot my tutor?*
—SHAKESPEARE, *The Tempest*

The curtain opens.

It is a sunny day.

In the back of the stage we see, as the stage backdrop, the façade of a farmhouse.

The stage is not deep.

The left side of the stage, from our vantage point, shows a view of a cornfield.

The right side of the stage, from our vantage point, is formed by a view of a large beetfield.

Birds are circling above both fields.

In front of the farmhouse we see a peculiar, longish object and ask ourselves what it might represent.

A rubber coat, black, covers the object partially; yet it does not fit like a glove, and so we cannot recognize what the object represents onstage.

To the right of the picture of the farmhouse door, from our vantage point, we notice a wooden block with a hatchet in it in front of a window; or rather, a large piece of wood is lying on the block, which is not quite level on the ground, and a hatchet is sticking in the piece of wood. Round about the chopping block we notice many pieces of chopped wood, and also, of course, chips and splinters, strewn about the stage floor.

On the chopping block, next to the large piece of wood with the hatchet sticking in it, we notice a cat: while the curtain opens the cat probably raises its head and subsequently does what it usually does, so that we recognize: the cat represents what it does.

Upon first glance, we have seen someone sitting next to the chopping block, on a stool: a figure.

Now, after having briefly taken in the other features of the stage, we turn back to this figure sitting on a stool in the sunshine in front of the picture of the house.

He—the figure is that of a male—is dressed in rural garb: that is, he is wearing blue coveralls over his pants; his shoes are heavy; on top, the person is wearing only an undershirt.

No tattoos are visible on his arms.

The person wears no covering on his head.

The sun is shining.

It is probably not necessary to mention explicitly that the person squatting on the stool in front of the picture of the house is wearing a mask. This mask covers half of his face— the upper part, that is—and is immobile. It represents a face which, moreover, evinces an expression of considerable glee, within limits, of course.

The figure on the stage is young—some recognize that this figure probably represents the ward.

The ward has his legs stretched out in front of him.

We see that he is wearing hobnail boots.

The ward is holding the underside of his right knee with his left hand; the right leg, in contrast to the left, is slightly bent.

We see that the ward is leaning with his back against the backdrop representing the house wall.

In his right hand the figure is holding a rather large yellow apple. Now that the curtain has opened and is open, the figure brings the apple to his mouth.

The ward bites into the apple, as if no one were watching.

The apple does not crunch especially, as if no one were listening.

The picture as a whole exudes something of the quality of what one might call profound peacefulness.

The ward eats the apple, as if no one were watching.

(If you make a point to watch, apples are often eaten with a good deal of affectation.)

The figure thus consumes the apple, not particularly slowly, not particularly quickly.

The cat does what it does. If it should decide to leave the stage, no one should stop it from doing so.

If at first we paid too much attention to the figure, we now have sufficient time to inspect the other objects and areas (see above).

Can one gather from the manner in which the ward consumes the apple that he enjoys dependent status? Actually not.

Because we have been looking so intently, we have almost overlooked that the figure has already finished eating the apple. Nothing unusual has occurred during this process, the figure has no unusual way of consuming apples, perhaps a few seeds have fallen on the floor; chickens are not in evidence.

Now it's the second apple's turn.

To accomplish this, the ward stretches out his right leg completely, and with his left hand reaches under the coveralls into the right pocket of his pants. Obviously he is not making out too well.

He couldn't reach into the pocket with his right hand, however, since he would have to lean back to do so but sits too near the wall to be able to lean back as far as he would have to.

He slides forward with the stool and leans back against the picture of the wall: no, the upper and lower parts of his body are still at too much of an angle for his hand to be able to do what it wants to do.

The pause is noticeable.

The ward stands up and while he stands reaches into his pants pocket and easily extracts the apple.

While still in the process of sitting down, he bites into the apple.

With his bottom the ward shoves the stool closer to the wall of the house again and assumes a similar, though not precisely the same, position as the initial one; the cat moves or does not move, the ward eats.

From behind the cornfield backdrop—from our vantage point, the left—a second figure emerges, the warden, judging from all visible evidence: rubber boots covered with mud up to the knee, gray work pants, a checkered shirt (white & blue) with rolled-up sleeves, tattoos on his arms, an open collar, a mask covering the upper half of his face, a hat with a pheasant feather stuck in it, an insignia on the hat, a carpenter's pencil behind his ear, a very big pumpkin in front of his stomach.

Now that the warden has entered the stage, we see that the backdrop representing the cornfield consists of many small movable parts which are falling back into their original positions . . . the cornfield is calming down, the birds are again circling on one and the same spot.

The warden sees the ward.

The warden steps up close and takes a look at the ward.

The ward is quietly eating his apple.

The warden's watching the ward drags on.

Gradually, as we watch, the eating of the apple also begins to drag on.

The longer the warden watches the ward, the more the eating of the apple is drawn out.

When the warden has stared down the ward, the latter stops eating the apple.

The pumpkin which the warden is holding in front of his stomach is, as we see, a real pumpkin.

But we hardly notice this any more, for after the warden has outstared the ward and the ward has simultaneously ceased eating his apple, which is now lying oddly half-eaten in the ward's hand, the stage is already becoming gradually dark. The scene is finished.

A new scene now begins in the dark, we can hear it. What we hear is a loud, prerecorded breathing that is piped in over a loudspeaker. After a period of silence the loud breathing suddenly sets in, and it continues neither evenly louder nor softer but constantly wavering back and forth within its prescribed decibel range, in such a manner that we are made to think: now it will get louder and louder and become the loudest possible breathing, but at this point it suddenly becomes quite soft again, and we think: now the breathing is about to stop altogether, when it suddenly becomes loud again, and in fact far louder than what we consider natural breathing. It is "like" the strongly amplified breathing of an old man, but not quite; on the other hand, it is "like" the strongly amplified breathing of a wild animal that has been cornered, but not quite, either; it is "voracious," "frightened," "ominous," but not quite; at times it seems to signify someone's "death throes" to us, but somehow it doesn't either because it appears to change location constantly. In the Italian spy film *The Chief Sends His Best Man* (with Stewart Granger and Peter van Eyck, directed by Sergio Sollima) there is a sequence in which an apartment—which someone has entered and in which he has found his dead friend—suddenly becomes dark; after a few moments of quiet the aforementioned breathing suddenly becomes audible all over the room, and for such a long time and so intensively that the intruder, in his desperation, starts shooting and jumps up from behind his chair, whereupon he is shot and the lights are turned on—a young man stands above him, a small tape recorder in his hand, which he now switches off, whereupon the "hideous" breathing stops: that is the kind of breathing that is meant here, without the same consequences, of course—as suddenly as it started, it stops again after a certain time.

We are sitting pretty much in the dark; judging from the noises coming from that direction, the stage is being rearranged.

While it is gradually becoming completely dark, we hear music, a succession of chords piped in very much at random, with the pauses between them varying in length. Occasionally several chords follow each other in quick succession.

The chords are taken from the tune "Colors for Susan" from *I Feel Like I'm Fixin' to Die* (Vanguard VSD 70266) by Country Joe and the Fish. The piece only lasts five minutes and fifty-seven seconds, so it's repeated over and over during the course of events, except for the very end of the tune, which is reserved for the end of the events.

Onstage, ward and warden are in the process of rearranging the stage: what was inside before is now turned inside out.

If the stage is of the revolving kind, this process is managed by turning the stage 180 degrees.

If the stage is not of the revolving kind, ward and warden simply turn the backdrops of the cornfield, beetfield, and house façade so that the backs of the backdrops now represent the inside walls of the house.

We look out through the back window, behind which the birds are circling.

Lacking a revolving stage, ward and warden take the objects that stood in front of the house (the object under the rubber coat, etc.) to the back of the stage, and now, as it becomes bright again, they bring the furnishings for the house onstage.

This is what is required for the play: a rather large table, two chairs, an electric hot plate, a coffee grinder, an assortment of bottles, glasses, cups, saucers, and plates (on the floor in back), an oil lamp, a rubber hose, a bootjack, a newspaper which sticks in the crack of the door.

On a nail on the door hangs a bullwhip; on the same nail there also hangs a pair of scissors.

We see a large monthly calendar hanging on what is, from our vantage point, the right wall of the room.

But so that we can see all of this, the following has transpired in the meantime: the warden lit a match in the dark and turned up the oil lamp. As we already know from many other plays, the entire stage gradually becomes bright when someone lights an oil lamp: the same happens here.

Now that the stage is brightly lit—let us not forget to listen to the music, which becomes neither softer nor louder—we see it in the following condition: it now represents the room of a house. But this room is still empty, except for the paper in the crack of the door, the objects on the door, and the calendar.

We see ward and warden, who come onstage from the left and right sides respectively, distribute the aforementioned objects throughout the room: each brings in a chair, then the table is brought onstage by the two of them, then comes the warden with the rubber hose, which he drags across the stage before dropping it, then comes the ward with the bottles and plates, then the warden with the glasses—unhurriedly but not ceremonially either—just as though we weren't watching; circus workers would go about it differently. No evincing of satisfaction, no contemplation of work well done, no moving to the music.

They both sit down, the ward almost first but he stops midway and the warden is seated, then the ward sits down too.

They both make themselves comfortable.

The music is pleasant.

The warden extends his legs under the table.

The ward also extends his legs under the table and comes to a halt when he touches the warden's feet; then, after a pause, the ward slowly withdraws his legs; the warden does not withdraw his.

The ward sits there. What to do with his legs?

Quiet, music.

The ward puts his feet on the front crosspiece of his own chair, and to accomplish this he uses his body to shove the chair back, producing the customary sound; the warden doesn't let himself be disturbed, he replies by taking off his hat and placing it on the table.

Quiet, music.

The ward slowly looks around the room, around, up, and also down, but avoids grazing the warden with his eyes, makes an about-face, so to speak, whenever he is just about to look at the warden: this is repeated so often that it loses its psychological significance.

The warden watches the ward.

The ward stands up, takes an apple from his pants pocket underneath the coveralls, and puts it beside the hat.

The warden lowers his gaze to the apple.

The ward starts gazing around the room again. What is there to see in the room?

Suddenly, as if he senses a trap, the warden cocks his head.

The ward, caught by the warden's gaze, stops looking around.

Mutual staring at each other, gazing, mutual looking through each other, mutual looking away. Each one looks at the other's ear.

The ward places both feet on the floor simultaneously; we can hear it.

The warden looks at the ward's ear.

The ward gets up carefully, softly.

The warden looks at him, at his ear.

The ward, aware only of himself, goes to the door, his steps, careful at first, becoming progressively louder as he approaches it.

The warden follows him with his eyes.

The ward bends down and pulls the newspaper out of the crack in the door.

The warden does not follow the ward with his eyes but keeps them fixed on the door: what's hanging on the door?

The ward straightens up, goes back to the table with the paper under his arm, walking progressively more carefully again, once by the table walking almost soundlessly; while underway he uses his free hand to take the paper from under his arm and holds it neatly in his hand by the time he stands before the table.

The warden gazes at the door.

The ward neatly places the paper beside the hat and the apple.

The warden lowers his head; in the pause between the movements we hear a louder chord.

The ward sits down without making a sound, sits the way he did before; the next chord is suddenly softer.

The warden unfolds the paper completely.

He reads. He folds the paper together to the size of one page. He pretends to read that page. He reads so that it is almost a pleasure to watch him reading.

The ward, while seated, pulls, with a good deal of effort, a tiny book out of his pants pocket, the same pants from which he produced the apples, and also reads and is no less pleasant to look at.

The warden folds the newspaper page in half and goes on reading.

The ward pulls a pencil out of his pants pocket, a carpenter's pencil like the warden's, only smaller; he uses it to mark in the book while reading.

The warden goes on folding the paper.

The ward no longer marks in his book but crosses something out.

The warden goes on folding as best he can.

The ward is obviously starting to draw in the little book.

The warden folds.

The ward exceeds the margins of the book while drawing and begins to draw on the palm of his hand.

The warden: see above.

The ward draws on the back of his hand.

The warden is gradually forced to start crumpling the paper, but we don't actually notice the transition from folding to crumpling.

The ward draws on his forearm; what he draws doesn't necessarily have to resemble the warden's tattoos.

The warden is obviously no longer reading or folding but is vigorously crumpling.

Both figures are vigorously occupied, one with drawing, the other with crumpling.

The warden completes the crumpling process and the paper is now a tight ball.

The ward is still drawing.

The warden is quiet, the ball of paper in his fist; he looks at his opposite, who is drawing.

The ward is drawing; the longer his opposite gazes at him, the more slowly he draws.

Then, instead of drawing, he merely scratches himself with the pencil and finally turns it around and scratches his arm with the other end; then he pushes the pencil into his arm without moving it. Then he stops doing this and slowly places the pencil next to the hat on the table; he quickly pulls his hand away and places it, slowly, on the forearm with the drawing on it.

The warden places his fist with the crumpled paper on the table and leaves it there.

The ward starts looking around the room once more, up, down, to the side, down along his legs.

The warden unclenches the fist holding the paper ball and places his hand next to it on the table; the paper ball slowly expands.

The music, noticeably louder now, is pleasant.

A period without movement—though that is not to say that the figures become graven images—now follows, unobtrusively introducing the next sequence.

During the period without movement we just listen to the music. Now the music becomes nearly inaudible, just as the main theme may disappear almost entirely during certain sections of a film.

We see the warden slowly place his forearms on the table.

In reply to this movement, the ward places his hands on the table, fingertips pointing at the warden.

The warden, without looking at the ward, slowly places his head on his forearms, on his hands, actually, and in such a way that his mouth and nose are placed on the backs of his hands, with his eyes looking across them.

Thereupon the ward slowly lowers his head toward the table until his head is hanging between his arms at the height of the table. After pausing briefly in this position and at this level, the ward lowers his head even further, down between his outstretched arms, which he has to bend now, until his head almost touches his knees: the ward remains in that position.

The warden draws his head toward himself until it lies, not with his mouth and nose, but with his forehead on his hands.

The ward spreads his knees and sticks his head deeper down between his bent arms and spread knees.

The warden pulls his hands out from under his head and now lies with his bare face, that is, with his bare mask, on the table.

(All these movements, although they occur very slowly, are not ceremonial.)

The ward lets his arms drop from the table but leaves his head hanging between his knees at the previous level.

The warden, while keeping his face in the previous position, uses his body to push the chair as far away from the table as possible, while still keeping his face on the table, his body slipping from the chair.

The ward, if possible, clenches his knees together above his head or against it.

Both of them are completely quiet onstage, as if no one were watching.

We hear the music somewhat more distinctly.

Some time passes; it has already passed.

The objects are in their places, here and there.

The warden stands up, without our noticing the in-between movements; he stands there, he represents standing, nothing else.

What will the ward do now?

Some time passes; we wait.

Now the ward sits up, without our particularly noticing the in-between movements.

What is the warden doing? He walks about the stage and represents walking.

The ward gets up; he stands there.

The warden runs; the ward begins to walk.

The warden leaps; the ward begins to . . .

The warden climbs up on a chair and is now standing on it; the ward does not leap but stops in his tracks and stands there.

The warden climbs on the table; the ward climbs on the chair.

The warden takes the other chair and puts it on the table and climbs on the chair on the table; the ward—how could it be otherwise?—climbs on the table.

The warden grabs on to a rope hanging down and hangs there; the ward climbs on the chair on the table.

The warden is hanging quietly, dangling a little, and the ward is quietly standing, high on the chair.

The warden lets himself drop. He lands with bent knees, then gradually straightens up to his full length.

The ward quickly climbs off the chair onto the table, from the table down onto the other chair, from this chair down onto the floor, and while doing so also takes the chair on the table down with him, putting it back in its old place and squatting down almost simultaneously.

All of this transpires so rapidly that if we wanted to count, we could hardly count further than one.

The warden slowly squats down.

The ward sits on the floor.

The warden slowly sits down also.

As soon as the warden sits down, the ward quickly lies down on the floor.

The warden slowly, ever so slowly, lies down on his back also, and makes himself comfortable.

As soon as the warden is lying on his back, the ward quickly rolls over and lies on his stomach.

The warden, emphasizing each of his movements with the sound it produces, also rolls over on his stomach, slowly.

As best he can, the ward now bends all his extremities together. We see him diminishing everywhere and becoming smaller. But he wasn't an inflated balloon before, was he? It appears that he was. The ward becomes smaller and smaller, and flatter, the stage becomes increasingly dark. The warden stays on his stomach as we last saw him, the stage is now dark, we hear the isolated chords.

The stage becomes bright.

We see that the two figures are again seated at the table in their previous positions.

The warden gets up, goes to the bootjack, takes off his boots in a completely professional manner, without exaggerating, as if no one were watching. He kicks each boot across the stage with one kick.

The ward gets up, goes where the boots are lying, and puts them next to each other beside the door.

One after the other, warden and ward go back to their places.

A brief pause.

The warden rolls his woolen socks from his feet and flings them, bunched up, across the stage, one here, the other there, without any evidence of nasty motives, just as if no one were watching.

The ward gets up, finds the socks, straightens them out, pulls them right side out, and places them as nicely as possible across the boots. Then he returns to the table and sits down.

The warden gets up, goes to the door, takes the scissors off the nail, and returns with the scissors to the table.

After sitting down, he places his naked foot on the side crosspiece of the chair and cuts his toenails.

We know the sounds.

He behaves as if we were not really watching.

He cuts his toenails so slowly and for such a long time that it no longer seems funny.

When he is finally done he places the scissors on his knees.

After some time the ward gets up and walks about the stage, picking up the clipped-off toenails and putting them in the palm of one hand.

He does this so slowly that it, too, is no longer a laughing matter.

When the ward finally straightens up and returns to the table, the warden takes the scissors from his knees and now begins to clip his fingernails.

The ward turns around and goes to the calendar hanging on the right-hand wall.

The warden cuts and the ward tears off a sheet from the calendar.

The warden cuts and . . .

The warden cuts and . . .

It is a slow process, without rhythm; it takes the warden a different amount of time to cut off each nail, and the ward needs a different amount of time to tear off each sheet from the calendar; the noises of the snipping and tearing overlap, are not necessarily successive, sometimes occur simultaneously; the calendar sheets flutter to the floor.

Now the calendar has been completely shorn: all we can see of it is the rather large empty cardboard backing left hanging on the wall.

But the warden is still cutting his fingernails, and the ward is standing inactively by the wall, his face half to the wall.

The music, which becomes more distinct, is so pleasant that the noise the scissors make hardly affects us.

And now that the stage is becoming dark the noise stops at once.


It becomes bright.

The two persons are sitting in their initial positions at the table, quietly, each by himself.

The warden gets up, goes to the hot plate. He takes the tea-kettle from behind the row of bottles and puts one end of the rubber hose into the kettle.

The warden exits, returns immediately.

We hear water running into the kettle.

The warden exits and returns at once.

He takes the hose out of the kettle, lets it drop. He puts the cover on the kettle and puts the kettle on the hot plate.

The warden drags the rubber hose onstage.

As the hose is apparently very long, he has to drag for quite a long time. Finally the warden drags the entire hose onstage.

Nothing funny happens.

He winds the hose in an orderly manner over hand and elbow, goes to the table, and places the rolled-up hose with the other objects on the table. He resumes his position.

Quietly, contemplating each other, the two figures squat onstage.

Gradually we begin to hear the water simmering in the kettle.

The noises we hear are those that are produced when water
„  „  „  „  „  „   „  „   „   „  „
„  „  „  „  „  „   „  „   „   „  „
is heated.
„   „
„   „

The ward gets up, fetches the coffee grinder, sits down, makes himself comfortable on the chair, clasps the coffee grinder between his knees and starts to grind. We can hear the grinding . . .

The ward is grinding, apparently unaware of anything
„  „  „  „   „   „   „  „
„  „  „  „   „   „   „  „
„  „  „  „   „   „   „  „
„  „  „  „   „   „   „  „
„  „  „  „   „   „   „  „
else . . .
„
„
„
„
„

The teakettle whistles . . .
„   „   „
„   „   „

The ward gradually stops grinding . . .
„  „   „   „   „
„  „   „   „   „
„  „   „   „   „

Now the stopper is probably blown off the kettle, so that it becomes quiet again.

The music sets in at the appropriate moment, when the stage once more becomes dark.

On the bright stage we see the two persons at the table, the hot plate having of course been turned off in the meantime.

The warden gets up and goes offstage.

But he returns quite soon, a frying pan with glowing incense in one hand, a big piece of white chalk in the other.

We smell the incense and also see clouds of incense.

The warden goes to the door and starts writing something on the top of the door.

The moment he puts chalk to wood, the ward turns toward him on the chair; the ward reaches into his pants and throws something at the warden . . . it must be something very light because the warden does not stop his very slow writing, which looks almost like drawing.

The ward makes himself comfortable on his chair and throws again, unhurriedly.

The warden writes; the ward throws.

We see that the ward's projectiles are sticking to the warden's shirt: yes, they are thistles.

While the warden is slowly writing, the ward occasionally throws a thistle at him, yet without expressing anything with the manner in which he throws it.

We hear the music and smell the incense.

The warden's back is slowly but surely covered with a cluster of thistles while he writes.

He writes slowly down along the door:

K + M + B
K + M + B
K + M + B
K + M + B
„     „     „

„     „     „

„     „     „

„     „     „

The ward now takes the thistles out of his fist and throws them with the other hand.

The warden, while writing, takes the bullwhip from the door.

Now he steps back.

The ward happens to be throwing again.

The warden turns around as though accidentally, not quickly; at the same time, the ward throws a thistle, which hits the warden's chest (or not). The warden is standing there by himself; the ward throws the remaining thistles at the warden.

The warden is holding the pan with the incense in front of him. The longer the warden holds the pan, the longer the intervals between the ward's throws.

Meanwhile, it gradually becomes dark once again, and the music . . . (see above)

The two figures are sitting on the stage, which is bright again; they are sitting at the table, each one by himself.

They are sitting, each one by himself.

```
"    "    "    "    "    "    "
"    "    "    "    "    "    "
"    "    "    "    "    "    "
"    "    "    "    "    "    "
```

All at once we notice there is blood running from the ward's nose. The blood trickles out of his nose, across his mouth, over his chin, out of his nose . . .

The warden is sitting there by himself, the ward doesn't budge from the spot, doesn't budge from the spot . . .

Gradually it becomes dark again on the stage.

Once we can see again, both of them are sitting in their positions at the table.

The ward gets up and stands against the rear wall, with his back to us.

The warden gets up, goes to the ward, grabs him by the shoulder, without expressing anything (that is, not violently), and turns him around.

The warden, after a pause, changes the position of his hands and turns the ward around once more.

The turning around gradually turns into turning around and turning around, now into turning around pure and simple.

The warden turns the ward with ease, almost as though he were thinking of something else, and the ward turns easily, also as though he were thinking of something else.

Without transition, without either of them staggering, we suddenly see the warden standing by the bottles and plates.

The ward has been standing still for some time before we really notice that he is standing still.

The warden has already bent down and while bending down throws a bottle toward the ward: the ward shows how he would like to catch but can't—the bottle falls on the floor and does what it does.

As one can imagine, it goes on like this: Bending down, the warden throws bottles, plates, and glasses toward the ward, but the ward, although apparently making an effort, lets all the objects fall on the floor, and the objects either break or they don't.

This process also lacks a regular rhythm: they wait now and then, then the warden throws once more, then the ward misses again . . .

Suddenly, even before the collection of bottles has been disposed of—amid the nicest possible throwing and breaking—the ward catches an object, as if by accident.

We are startled.

At the same moment the stage becomes dark, abruptly.

And again it becomes bright, and both of them are sitting at the table. The warden gets up and goes where? Apparently he doesn't know where he should go.

No, he doesn't want to go to the calendar.

He turns around, turns around, is turning around.

The ward gets up and walks after him; he shows how he shares the warden's indecision and imitates the warden's gestures, his leg movements as well as his indecisive arm movements, although the imitation need not be a complete aping.

They almost collide when the warden suddenly changes direction—he is probably avoiding the pieces of the broken bottles and plates; more than once the ward steps on the warden's heels. They continue moving about the stage, pretending to have a goal which, however, they never reach, because they always give it up just before they are about to reach it.

Suddenly the warden is by the door, is already going out, reaches for the outside door handle to shut the door behind him—the ward seizes the door handle on the inside, wants to follow the warden, but the warden pulls without letup.

The ward pulls in the other direction.

The warden, by giving one hard pull, pulls the door shut behind him and in front of the ward, who has been pulled along by the violent pull.

The ward stands briefly in front of the door, his hand around the handle, then his hand merely touching the handle.

The ward lets his hand drop.

The warden is outside; it is quiet.

The ward gets down on his knees, without falling down on them, however, and is already crawling out the door, quickly: we see now that the door has an extra outlet, as if for a dog.

Once the ward is outside, the stage slowly becomes dark.

By now we have become accustomed to the music.

The pause is longer this time, for the scenery is being turned inside out.

A revolving stage needs only to revolve.

Otherwise, the scenery is turned around in the dark.

It becomes bright: it is a rainy day.

Warden and ward set up the objects on the stage: the

large, longish object, covered by the black raincoat, which they have to bring onstage together, the stool, beets, melons, pumpkins.

When everything has been distributed on the stage, the ward sits down on the stool while the warden stands next to the mysterious object.

Without an actual beginning the play has begun again: the warden takes the rubber coat off the object, so that we see that it is a beet-cutting machine.

The warden puts on the raincoat (he is still barefoot) and, to test the machine, lets the cutting knife drop down several times without, however, cutting any beets.

The ward gets up and walks to the machine. The warden bends down for a beet, shoves it into the machine, and pulls down the cutting knife with one brief, effortless movement, as he indicates with a movement: the beet falls down, its top shorn off.

The warden repeats the process in detail, demonstrating: another beet falls down.

The ward watches, not completely motionless, but without moving very much.

The warden repeats the process.

The ward fetches a beet but makes many superfluous movements and detours; we can hear his hobnail boots on the floor as well as the bare feet of the warden, who now goes to the side and straightens up.

The ward raises the cutting knife, shoves the beet up to its top into the machine, and hacks off the top.

The warden steps up to him, stands beside him, steps back again . . .

The ward goes and fetches a few beets and puts them into place . . .

The warden steps up to him and stands there.

The cat suddenly slinks out of the house.

The ward's next attempt to cut off the top of a beet is so feeble that the beet does not fall on the floor at once.

The warden stands there watching him.

With the next attempt, the beet falls on the floor.

The cat does what it does.

The warden stands there.

The ward has problems with the beet again: he makes one attempt to sever its top, a second one, and then, without looking at the warden, who is starting to walk about the stage once more in his bare feet, a third attempt; then, after a certain time, when the warden is standing next to him again and is watching him, once more; then, later—it is already becoming darker on stage—a fifth time (the warden is starting to walk again); then—it is already quite dark (is the warden standing by the machine?)—finally once more, and now —we can't bear watching it any more—once again, and we don't hear the sound of anything falling on the floor; thereupon it is quiet onstage, for quite some time.

After it has been quiet onstage for some time we hear, quite softly at first, a breathing that becomes increasingly louder. We recognize it. It becomes louder, that is, larger and larger—a death rattle? A very intense inhaling? Or only a bellows? Or a huge animal?

It becomes steadily louder.

Gradually it becomes too large for the house.

Is it here, is it over there?

Suddenly it is quiet.

After a long time it becomes bright again.

The house, the cornfield, the beetfield.

We see neither the cat, nor the warden, nor the ward; not even the beet-cutting machine remains onstage—except for the three backdrops, it is bare.

Now someone enters from the right: it is the ward.

He is carrying a small tub in front of him, and wound about his upper body is a rubber hose.

He is no longer wearing his coveralls.

The tub is placed on the floor, the hose is unrolled.

One end of the hose is placed in the tub; the ward takes the other end offstage, straightening the hose in the process.

We hear the water running into the tub for some time.

Then the ward returns, a sack of sand in one arm.

He puts the sack next to the tub.

He reaches into the sack with his hand.

He straightens up and lets a handful of sand fall into the tub, without letting the sand slip between his fingers first.

He again reaches into the sack and, standing, lets a handful of sand fall into the water.

He again reaches into the sack and, standing, lets a handful of sand fall into the water, nonchalantly, irregularly, unceremoniously.

He again reaches into the sack and, standing, lets a handful of sand fall into the water.

Now we hear the isolated chords again.

The ward reaches into the sack and, standing, lets a hand-
The ward reaches into the sack and, standing, lets a hand-
The ward reaches into the sack and, standing, lets a hand-
,,    ,,     ,,      ,,   ,,   ,,   ,,      ,,     ,,   ,,   ,,
,,    ,,     ,,      ,,   ,,   ,,   ,,      ,,     ,,   ,,   ,,
,,    ,,     ,,      ,,   ,,   ,,   ,,      ,,     ,,   ,,   ,,
,,    ,,     ,,      ,,   ,,   ,,   ,,      ,,     ,,   ,,   ,,

ful of sand fall into the water.
ful of sand fall into the water.
ful of sand fall into the water.
,,   ,,   ,,   ,,   ,,   ,,   ,,
,,   ,,   ,,   ,,   ,,   ,,   ,,
,,   ,,   ,,   ,,   ,,   ,,   ,,
,,   ,,   ,,   ,,   ,,   ,,   ,,

We hear both, the chords and the sand falling into the
,,   ,,   ,,   ,,   ,,   ,,   ,,   ,,   ,,   ,,   ,,
,,   ,,   ,,   ,,   ,,   ,,   ,,   ,,   ,,   ,,   ,,
,,   ,,   ,,   ,,   ,,   ,,   ,,   ,,   ,,   ,,   ,,
,,   ,,   ,,   ,,   ,,   ,,   ,,   ,,   ,,   ,,   ,,
,,   ,,   ,,   ,,   ,,   ,,   ,,   ,,   ,,   ,,   ,,

water, as the stage gradually becomes dark.

```
"    "    "    "         "         "      "
"    "    "    "         "         "      "
"    "    "    "         "         "      "
"    "    "    "         "         "      "
"    "    "    "         "         "      "
```

The curtain closes.

**Translated by Michael Roloff**

*Quodlibet*

## Translator's note

More than any of Handke's plays to date, Quodlibet (*written in 1969, between* Kaspar *and* The Ride Across Lake Constance) *requires fairly extensive adaptation to an American linguistic, cultural, and historical environment. Why this is necessary is made apparent by the play itself. What finally surprised me, though, was the comparative ease with which indigenously German allusions—allusions to the various manifestations, public and private, of fascism—can be replaced by American equivalents. In further adaptations, which a cast may want to make, it would be worthwhile to consult the invectives at the end of Handke's* Offending the Audience (Publikumsbeschimpfung) *simply to see how "not to overdo it." This translation is meant as a basic model for American productions.*

M.R.

The curtain rises. On the bare stage, one by one, talking quietly to each other, appear the figures of the "world theater": a general in uniform, a bishop in his vestments, a dean in his gown; a Maltese knight in the coat of his order; a member of a German student corps with his little cap and sash; a Chicago gangster with his fedora and pin-striped double-breasted suit, a politician with two heavily armed CIA bodyguards; a dance-contest couple—he in a dark suit and white turtleneck sweater, she in a short, pert dress; a grande dame in a long evening gown, carrying a fan; another female figure in a pants suit, a poodle on the leash.

These figures come on stage in no particular order, separately or in pairs, arm in arm or not. Chatting, they slowly walk about the stage, step here and there, laugh softly at some remark or other, walk on again, not that one hears them walking of course. Each chats with the others at some point; every so often one of them stands apart alone as though struck suddenly by some thought before starting a new conversation; only the bodyguards take no part in the conversations; they nod to each other occasionally, that's all; otherwise they keep peering away from the figures on stage into the surrounding area, once up into the rigging loft, then—this without bending down—into the prompter's box, then into the vault of the theater as though up into the fifth tier of an opera house—at any event, never at the audience itself: the audience does not exist for the figures on the stage. One notices that all the figures briefly come to a complete stop, but the next moment one or two are walking again. At moments the general conversation almost lapses into complete silence; there are also moments during which only the rustling of garments on the floor is audible, whereafter the conversation resumes more vociferously and insistently than before.

The figures walk about making almost no sound, lost in themselves, stand still, are still, chat: that's actually all there is to it. It's entirely up to the actors what they want to say. They can talk about what they've just read in the papers, what they've experienced that day, what they want to experience, about what just occurred to them, or about something that gives the impression of having just occurred to them . . . a few times one thinks one hears them speaking a foreign language, probably French: C'est très simple, Monsieur.—Ah merci . . . oh! ma coiffure! . . . Ah! Ce vent! . . . Cette pluie! . . . Or something of that kind, invariably uttered by the women. The audience of course strains to listen, but only occasionally gets a few words, or snatches of sentences.

Among the words and sentences that the audience does understand—besides the irrelevant and meaningless ones like "Do you understand?" "Not that I know," "Why not?" "As I said," "And you?"—are some which the audience merely thinks it understands. These are words and expressions which in the theater act like bugle calls: political expressions, expressions relating to sex, the anal sphere, violence. Of course the audience does not really hear the actual expressions but only similar ones; the latter are the signal for the former; the audience is bound to hear the right ones. For example, instead of *napalm* they mention *no palms* onstage; instead of *Hiroshima* they speak of a *hero sandwich*; instead of *cun-*

*nilingus of cunning fingers;* instead of *psychopath* of *bicycle path;* instead of *leathernecks* of *leather next;* instead of *Auschwitz* of *house wits;* instead of *dirty niggers* of *dirty knickers* . . . Or the actors use double-edged words in sentences with invariably harmless connotations, but in such quick succession that one listens to the ambiguous words instead of the sentences, for example: *thigh, prick, member, spread, panties, tear, pant, cancer, victim, fag, rag, paralysis, stroke, frag* . . . Many sentences, which appear to be quite harmless, are also uttered in quick succession; however, they contain words which, when they appear in clusters, begin to give the illusion of an allusion: A sentence with the words *tiger cage* ("I didn't want to put my tiger in the cage but the cops insisted.") is followed by a sentence containing the word *gook* ("I wasn't completely satisfied until I had wiped the gook off the wall."), which is followed by a sentence with the word *waste* ("Sad to say, but we had to waste a lot of . . . time"), which is followed by a sentence containing the words *anti-personnel weapon* ("Anti-Americanism is a weapon I personally refuse to use."), which is followed by a sentence with the word *infrastructure* ("The infrastructure of the organization, if I may say so, consists of living bodies, all you have to do is count them"), which of course also contains the words *body count* in slightly different form, and which is followed by a sentence containing a distorted form of the words *Tonkin Gulf & Saigon* ("Tom's kinfolk made a resolution not to take the Gulf Line steamer to *Saigon.*") and finally a sentence containing the proper name *My Lai,* also in distorted form because of the proximity of the event ("As the old bastard of an Irishman used to say to me about Dora: 'She was me last lay before me prostate operation, and she was me very best lay.'").

The *hit* turns out to be a *two-run hit,* the *beating* is a *beating around the bush,* the *bomb* turns out to be *what a bomb this play was,* the *smashed brain on the stone* turns into *mashed potatoes alone,* where someone *spread blood* it turns out that the *old beer-belly actually sweated Bud;* when *shot* is mentioned it only refers to a *shot* of *whiskey;* and what *shot through his head* were only *thoughts;* "Shot through the head!"—"Shot through the head?"—"Yes, thoughts shot through my head." *Syphilis* is *Sisyphus* & *the clap* is a *thunderclap* & a *dildo* becomes *dill does it too.*

"Cashes in!"—"Cashes in pretty good!"—"The cops?"—"By the cops!"—"Cashed in?"

". . . broken!"—"with grief . . ."—"The neck?"—"A bottle!"—". . . the neck!"—"Broken . . ."—". . . and stuck the finger in . . ."—"Good!"—"Cut off!"—"What kind of head?"—"The conversation?"—"What?"—"He's one good head shorter."—"Off."—"What kind of head?"—"Good, good."

". . . three, four:"—"One, two, three—go!"—"One, two, three, four, five, six, seven . . ."—"One, two, three, four, five, six, seven (*pause*) eight (*pause*) nine (*pause*) ten—finished!" "Once, once more, a third time, four times, five times, and once more . . ."—"And then it was already getting bright outside . . ."—"Twenty-one, twenty-two—it's uncanny, uncanny."—"And then I stopped counting . . ."

"Corpses in quiet waters . . ."—"Oh, what a pretty title"—"Like an O?"—". . . laying their eggs there."—"Like *Story of O?*"—"As *though* it were nothing . . ."—"Shame!"—". . . 'and didn't say a single word!' "—"What a beautiful title!"—"Oh!"—". . . the carps lay their eggs in quiet waters . . ."—"In Lake Erie?"—"Shame! shame! and shame once more!"—"Let's say it was nothing!"—"According to the Geneva convention, o.k.?"

"The project died . . ."—" 'Dying' is a typo, actually it should say 'dried'!"—"Of fear?"—"A projectile with a crossnotch at the tip . . ."—"Quietly!"—"Died?"—"Very quietly!"—"I'm dying."—"What was the name of that bar?"—"Dum-Dum!"—"Of laughter?"—"I can't go on!"—"Blood?"—"Into the blood!"—"As for me, he died!"—"Died for all of us . . ."—"Quiet!"—"Psst!"—"Silence!"—(*silence*)—"An angel walked through the room!"—"Oh, Harlem . . . !"—"Yes."

—"Unforgettable those tulip fields!"—"Haarlem . . ."—
"Yeasz . . ."

". . . shaking with fear!"—"Pardon the question: 'Shaking with fear'?"—Someone else in the background: ". . .
shake well before use!"—"Excuse me!"

". . . could be seen from far away: fucked the cows . . ."
—"Fucked?"—"Forgot the cows, John Wayne. I believe, I
forgot the name of the film."—Someone farther away:
"Knocked out her teeth!"—"Who knocked her up?"—And
someone even farther away: "Knocked them down with
bombs."

Continuing at once: "Rammed a rod up his ass!"—Louder:
"Ramrods have passed."—Quite comprehensible but not too
loud, recited negligently like verse: ". . . rambling through
the brambles of glass . . . / . . . roaring through the rip-
tide of grass . . ." To his partner: "Do you still remember?"
The partner lowers his or her head, smiles, and walks on:
"Whether W. C. Fields slipping freely . . ." The first one,
more softly: "Sipping."—Even more softly: "What simper-
ing?" The sound of someone becoming louder emanates
from an altogether different spot: ". . . . chalice of sor-
row . . ." Now the first of the two partners walks on smiling.
And on: "And a bit of spit on the fly which . . ." The lady
with the fan in the background.—"Yes, the tits of my girl
Friday." One thereupon thinks one hears one of the two
partners saying.—"No, a dog that bit off my clitoris(?) . . ."

While stepping-slowly-forward: ". . . and I tasted . . ."
Correcting himself while approaching: ". . . which tasted
me . . ."—". . . tasted the soft inside of a . . . cyst . . ."—
In front by the footlights, humming elatedly with lowered
head: ". . . a foretaste of heaven . . ."—A character who is
just walking past the lady with the fan says: "Tested me to the
utmost," and one thinks one can still hear the lady with the
fan's partner say—one can't really make out who is speaking—
while the two are edging into the background: ". . . cash his
cut . . . taste buds . . . spit and polish . . . soft insides got

sick . . . fucked watery corpses at Easter . . ." while all around on the stage many other characters are walking around chatting, though more softly, and smiling.

Then they recount: " 'Cold,' he said, 'cold, completely cold.' "—" 'Ice,' as she used to say then."—" 'Like a glance out of a ranch house in Nebraska,' they told us."—" 'Where the train got stuck in the snow,' she wrote back to me."—" 'Indescribably white!' she exclaimed."—" 'No!' he screamed."— " 'Light, nothing but light!' she squealed like a pig on a spit."—"He cabled: 'In the chest-high snow where the two, who had become snowblind in the meantime, were surrounded by St. Bernards . . .' "—"And I replied: 'And what are you?' "—" 'Put in cold storage,' I still understood, then the line went dead."—" 'A mouse?' I couldn't resist asking."— " 'For New Year's Eve in the fridge!' he wrote in so many words though the stamp allowed room for one more."—"The note said in Gothic script: 'Born dead . . .' "—" 'The ice pick already lodged in his head,' I read, 'he still bit his murderer's hand.' "—Someone then produces a poor imitation of the sound of "croaking," a chocking noise with the gums— *kch*—and his female partner emits a quick light laugh.

For a short while one hears the characters leave out one word in their sentences and sees them casting significant and conspiratorial glances at each other: "You remember how (*smirking and nodding of heads*) . . . used take lonely walks with his dog?"—"I don't need to tell you that . . . held different opinions on the matter."—"I often thought of . . . when I sat in my deck chair."—"When the radio announcer says . . . I drop everything at once."—"For days after . . . had squeezed my hand my whole body would break out in hives."—"I can't forget how . . . dangled on his suspenders on the hotel room door."—"It's unthinkable that . . . would have gone out on the street without his umbrella."—"What would have been different if . . . had succeeded in getting a hit at that time?"—"Not only when I sat on Plymouth Rock did I have to cry about what . . . told me about death."—"I often worry myself nearly to death whether Paraguay is really the right place for . . ."—"Usually one glance by a dark-eyed foreigner in an Indonesian restaurant is enough and I can't breathe any more and only see . . . (*outraged recollection*) in front of me—how he suddenly stepped out from behind the column toward (*melancholy recollection*) . . ."

Or they use the wrong instead of the correct word under the assumption that they understand each other anyway. "One should herd them together and then—'treat them to a good meal!'" (*Smirking and gentle laughter.*)—"Go after them—'and slap them on the shoulder!'"—". . . because his 'shirt tail' hung out of his 'door' . . ."—". . . When she came up to me and told me that I could 'visit' her."—"All I had to do was 'smile' at him and blood began pouring from his nose."—". . . grabbed between his legs to help him 'get upstairs.'"—"His dentures fell out of his mouth even before I'd 'said a single word.'"—"The 'slight draft' when we entered the room was enough for him to catch his death of cold."—"Up on the platform 'I kissed him on the forehead,' so that he suddenly lost his balance."—"Drove him, 'drove him out of his wits.'"—"Got caught in the fan belt and— 'woke up!'"—"I sent him a 'get-well card' registered mail and the man thanked me and dropped dead!"—"He aimed at— 'progress and change!'"—". . . I tried putting the 'cookie' in his mouth!!"—"Across the barbed wire—'into the soft moss of the Okefenokee, . . .'"—"Cut a 'piece of bread' off for him!"—". . . will give her a teaspoonful of 'cinnamon,' 'to taste!'"—". . . so that these bastards will let her 'come.'"

Then one of the figures in the background tells a joke of which again one only hears the key words, such as "then he said," "the second time," "again nothing"; all the other characters except maybe for two or three and the bodyguards are assembled around the narrator at this point. They listen quietly and finally, each in his own way, smile quietly to themselves, scream with laughter, shake their heads in puzzlement, inhale deeply (one of them perhaps out of turn), and then continue to circle about the stage.

From the conversations one has also managed to pick out with increasing frequency sentences which a figure speaks with a slightly raised though not overly excited voice: sentences from the repertoire of politicians when they are forced to defend themselves against catcalls from the audience, and which are useful to them as defense against interjections from the audience but are employed even when there are no interjections. For example: "Anyone who shouts shows that he doesn't have anything to say." "I would die to defend your right to speak, but would you do the same for me?" "What you don't have in your head gets stuck in your throat." "Your parents don't seem to have brought you up to let other people finish what they are saying." "Take one look at these characters and you get a permanent itch in your trigger finger." "I won't take back one iota of what I said." "Our economic accomplishments give us the right not to be constantly reminded of the past." "Oh, I see the lady is a gentleman!" "Those people with their caveman feelings and their Stone Age laughter want to set back our discussion by a thousand years." "You don't even notice how useful you are to us!" "Long hair and dirty fingernails are no proof that you're right!" "Just take one look at them, that's what they all look like!" "All I say is: Stalin, Stalin, Stalin!" "There's only one weapon against radicalism, and that's the vote." "They should first condemn the torture of the prisoners in North Vietnam." "We are controlled by the iron law of history." Plus what other set rejoinders of this kind exist [campaign speeches contain some rich pickings.—Trans.]. Not that the characters exaggerate them or address them directly to the audience or someone particular in the audience—rather, they speak them as asides, almost in a monologue, quietly and with finality, while they walk about the stage in their state of extraordinarily malicious and melancholy solitude. If someone fails to recognize this, and wants to join them on the stage, the bodyguards gently and without hurting him or her should lead the person off. To let the person remain on stage would only be a show of disdain.

While all characters begin to busy themselves more and more with themselves—stroking their hair, forehead, cheeks, lips; cracking their joints, picking lint off their clothes, slapping themselves on their arms, stomach, neck, and throat, stopping occasionally to tug at their earlobes—one also hears fragments of monologues which keep breaking off or become inaudible, as though the speakers were ashamed of what they were saying: ". . . I decided to join the company as a silent partner . . ."—"Last night I dreamed of Arizona . . ."— ". . . I saw the people's faces change color in the completely sold-out stadium . . ."—". . . I wrapped the boa around my neck and winked at him like Jane . . ."—". . . I suddenly saw a landscape as quiet and dreamlike as the transparent wing of a butterfly . . ."—". . . I kept the option of taking further steps . . ."—". . . at that time when I slipped off a pile of logs in my dream . . ."—(*A lady slowly raises her dress, beneath which she is completely naked, and slowly lets it fall again.*) ". . . and I heard my baby sister sighing in the kitchen . . ."—As though remembering, a few characters shake their heads one after the other and walk on. And while they are already walking again one of them says: ". . . while I was about to fall asleep I saw two hanged men dangling from one noose . . ."

For some time, that is, at least until the audience begins to pay attention, the characters move quietly around the stage like this, with their belt buckles, their collar patches, brooches and rings glinting in the muted light. Then while the chatter gradually subsides, because more and more characters stop talking, one can still hear one of them say: "What, when the pain becomes unbearable you want to simply waste them like animals?" And another replies: "Yes, should animals be any worse off than human beings?" And a little later someone else: "Yes, if I'd defended him at the trial, he might even have been able to wriggle his way out." And after the chatter has even further subsided—only now does one notice how heavily made up the characters are—the lady with the fan says softly but distinctly: "Even before he touched me I began to cream." And the two bodyguards, who stand quite far away, exchange obscene gestures. One pushes his thumb out between the middle and index finger of a closed fist; the other immediately replies by making a fist and whopping quickly up and down on the other fist. From the lady with the lapdog one hears, already as a memory, a pretty, long-drawn-out "Ahh . . ." and at this point it becomes gradually dark on stage and the curtain drops.

**Translated by Michael Roloff**

# The Ride Across Lake Constance

*It's a winter night. A man rides across Lake Constance without sparing his horse. When he arrives on the other side, his friends congratulate him profusely, saying: "What a surprise! How did you ever make it! The ice is no more than an inch thick!" The rider hesitates briefly, then drops off his horse. He is instantly dead.*

M.R.

## Characters

WOMAN WITH WHITE SCARF
EMIL JANNINGS
HEINRICH GEORGE
ELISABETH BERGNER

ERICH VON STROHEIM
HENNY PORTEN
ALICE AND ELLEN KESSLER
A DOLL

*To avoid character designations such as "Actor A," "Actor B," "Actress C," and so on, for reading and other purposes the characters in the play have been given the names of well-known actors.*

*When the play is staged, the characters should bear the names of the actors playing the roles: the actors are and play themselves at one and the same time.*

"Are You Dreaming or Are You Speaking?"

*The stage is large. It displays a section of an even larger room. The background is formed by the back wall of this room; the wall is covered by a brownish-green tapestry with a barely perceptible pattern. Along the back wall two parts of a staircase lead down from the right and left and meet in the center of the wall, where they form a single set of wide stairs, of which a number of steps lead forward into the room. The audience therefore sees persons walking down the stairs first in profile, then from the front. In the wall beneath the right and left parts of the stairway are two barely visible tapestry doors. The staircase has a delicately curved, slender bannister. The floor of the room is covered with an unobtrusive carpet whose color matches the tapestry; a wine-red runner leads down the staircase steps.*

*Most of the furnishings in the room are covered with drop-cloths; these are extremely white. In the center of the room, not precisely center of course, rather almost downstage, stands a large dark table, partially covered by a lace table-cloth; on it are an ashtray, a cigar box, a teapot or coffee pot covered with an embroidered cozy, a longish cutlery case, also of embroidered cloth, and two candlesticks sheathed in protective covers. To the right and left and behind the table stand three fauteuils with white dropcloths; next to and behind them are an easy chair and a straight chair, dropcloths over both. In front of one of the fauteuils stands a stool upholstered the same and the same height as the fauteuil that may serve as a footrest; a smaller footstool stands in front of the second fauteuil; the third fauteuil stands by itself. To the right of the table, a few steps away, stands a small bar, not covered, with several bottles whose forms indicate their respective contents. To the left of the table, a few steps away, stands a newspaper table, not covered either, with a few bulky magazines, some of which are still rolled up; on top is a record player with a record on it. Looking further to the left and right behind the newspaper table and bar one sees two sofas, also concealed by white dropcloths. To the left side of the left sofa is a brown-stained chest, with several drawers; on it a small statue covered with a white paper bag. On the right side of the right sofa leans a guitar in a bag embroidered like the tea cozy. Beneath the sections of the staircase hang two pictures on the wall concealed behind white sheets. Downstage to the extreme right, in line with the table, is a Japanese screen of the kind one usually sets up in front of beds. It is small and has three panels; two of them are slightly pushed together, the third is open and visible to the audience. The screen has the same pattern and color as the back wall.*

*All objects are in such a position that it would be difficult to imagine them standing elsewhere; it is as though they could not bear being moved ever so slightly. Everything appears as though rooted to the spot, not only the objects themselves but also the distances and empty spaces between them.*

*The light is that of early morning.*

*After the curtain has opened, two portieres to the right and left of the proscenium are revealed, as portieres to a* chambre séparée.

*A* woman, *her hair wrapped in a* white scarf, *moves*

quickly but not hastily among the objects with a vacuum cleaner. She is in blackface. The vacuum cleaner, which was turned on the moment the curtain began to open, makes a more or less steady noise.

On a fauteuil beside the table, his legs on the appropriate footstool, sits EMIL JANNINGS, his eyes closed. He is quite fat. His boots stand next to the stool. He is wearing red silk socks, black pants, a light-colored shirt, open at the collar. He seems costumed although only hints of a costume are visible: rather long frills on the sleeves of the silk shirt, a wine-red silk sash around his stomach.

He is heavily made up, the eyebrows are painted. On the right hand, whose nails are lacquered black, he wears several large rings.

He has not moved since the curtain opened, and the WOMAN has nearly completed her work. Pushing the vacuum cleaner back and forth near the newspaper table with one hand, she turns on the record player with the other.

However, one hears only a few isolated sounds; the vacuum cleaner is too noisy.

She takes the cleaner to the back wall and turns it off so that the music becomes audible: "The Garden Is Open" by T. Kupferberg. She pulls the plug out of the socket, rolls it up on the machine, and places the machine behind the tapestry door.

While the record continues to play, she walks from object to object and takes off the dropcloths, except those on the paintings and on the statue. Although she moves fairly slowly, her work is proceeding quite rapidly; at least, one barely notices it. She pulls the cover from under EMIL JANNINGS with a single movement and walks off to the left while the record is still playing.

Then nothing moves onstage for a while except for the record.

The record player turns itself off, and after a moment JANNINGS slowly opens his eyes.

JANNINGS
(*With a cracked voice*) As I said—(*He clears his throat once and repeats in a firm voice.*) As I said. (*Pause.*) A bad moment. (*Someone behind the screen with a cracked voice:* "Why?" *He clears his throat twice; the second time he does so he steps out from behind the screen, repeats then in a firm voice:* "Why?" *It is* HEINRICH GEORGE, *quite fat, his clothes also suggesting a costume, with braids trimming his jacket and with lace-up shoes. He stands there.* JANNINGS *has turned his head away slightly.*) It's over already.

GEORGE
(*Takes a step toward* JANNINGS *and collapses. As he slowly rises again*) My foot has fallen asleep.

JANNINGS
(*Reaches for the cigar box. He lifts it but cannot hold on to it so that it falls to the floor.*) So has my hand. (GEORGE *carefully walks up to* JANNINGS, *stops next to him. Both of them glance at each other for the first time, then look away again.* GEORGE *leans against the edge of the table, now sits down on it. The cigar box is lying on the floor between them. Both look at it.* JANNINGS *turns his head toward* GEORGE. GEORGE *slides off the table.* JANNINGS *points at the cigar box.* GEORGE *misunderstands the gesture and looks as if there was something to see on the box.* JANNINGS *agrees to the misunderstanding and now points as if he really wanted to point out something.*) That blue sky you see on the label, my dear fellow, it really exists there.

GEORGE
(*Bends down to the cigar box, takes it, looks at it.*) You're right! (*He puts the box back on the floor and straightens up.*)

JANNINGS
You're standing . . .

GEORGE
(*Interrupts him.*) I can also sit down. (*He sits down in the fauteuil with the smaller footstool and makes himself comfortable.*) What did you want to say?

JANNINGS
"You're standing just now: would you be kind enough to hand me the cigar box from the floor?"

(*Pause.*)

GEORGE
You were dreaming?

JANNINGS
When the nights were especially long, in winter.

GEORGE
You must be dreaming.

JANNINGS
Once, on a winter evening, I was sitting with someone in a restaurant. As I said, it was evening, we sat by the window and were talking about a corpse; about a suicide who had leaped into the river. Outside, it rained. We held the menus in our hands. "Don't look to the right!" (GEORGE *quickly looks to the left, then to the right.*) shouted the person opposite me. I looked to the right: but there was no corpse. Besides, my friend had meant I should not look on the right page of the menu because that was where the prices were marked. (*Pause.*) How do you like the story?

GEORGE
So it was only a story?

(*Pause.*)

JANNINGS
When one tells it, it seems like that to oneself.

GEORGE
Like a story? (JANNINGS *nods. Pause. Then he slowly shakes his head.*) So you're wrong after all. Then it's true what you told me?

JANNINGS
I'm just wondering.

(*Pause.*)

GEORGE
And how did it go on?

JANNINGS
We ordered kidneys flambé.

GEORGE
And you got them?

JANNINGS
Of course.

GEORGE
And asked for the check and got it?

JANNINGS
Naturally.

GEORGE
And asked for the coats and got them?

JANNINGS
Why the coats?

GEORGE
Because it was a winter evening.

JANNINGS
(*Relieved*) Of course.

GEORGE
And then?

JANNINGS
We went home.

(*Both laugh with relief. Pause.*)

GEORGE
Only one thing I don't understand. Of what significance is the winter evening to the story? There was no need to mention it, was there? (JANNINGS *closes his eyes and thinks.*) Are you asleep?

JANNINGS
(*Opens his eyes.*) Yes, that was it! You asked me whether I was dreaming and I told you how long I sleep during winter nights and that I then begin to dream toward morning, and as an example I wanted to tell you a dream that might occur during a winter night.

GEORGE
Might occur?

JANNINGS
I invented the dream. As I said, it was only an example. The sort of thing that goes through one's head . . . As I said— a story . . . `

GEORGE
But the kidneys flambé?

JANNINGS
Have you ever had kidneys flambé?

GEORGE
No. Not that I know.

JANNINGS
If you don't know, then you haven't had them.

GEORGE
No.

JANNINGS
You're disagreeing with me?

GEORGE
Yes, that is: no. That is: yes, I agree with you.

JANNINGS
In other words, when you mention kidneys flambé, you talk about something you know nothing about.

GEORGE
That's what I wanted to say.

JANNINGS
And about something one doesn't know, one shouldn't talk, isn't that so?

GEORGE
Indeed.

(JANNINGS *makes the appropriate gesture with his hand, turning up his palm in the process.* GEORGE *stares at it, and under the impression that* GEORGE *has found something on the palm* JANNINGS *leaves it like that. The hand now looks as if it is waiting for something; say, for the cigar box. After what has been said just now the hand has the effect of an invitation, so that* GEORGE *bends down and puts the box in* JANNINGS's *hand.*

*A brief pause, as if* JANNINGS *had expected something else. Then he takes the box with his other hand and puts it on his knee. He looks at his hand, which is still extended.*)

JANNINGS
That's not what I meant to say with that. It just seemed to me that you had noticed something on my hand. (*He opens the box top with his other hand and offers the box to* GEORGE, *who looks inside.*) Take one.

(GEORGE *quickly takes a cigar.* JANNINGS *takes one too.* GEORGE *takes the box from* JANNINGS *and puts it back on the table. Each lights his own cigar. Both lean back and smoke.*)

GEORGE
Haven't you noticed anything?

JANNINGS
Speak. (*Pause.*) Please, go ahead and speak.

GEORGE
Didn't you notice how silly everything suddenly became when we began to talk about kidneys flambé? No, not so much suddenly as gradually, the more often we mentioned the kidneys flambé. Kidneys flambé, kidneys flambé, kidneys flambé! And didn't it strike you why the kidneys flambé gradually made everything so hair-raisingly silly?

(*Pause.*)

JANNINGS
Speak.

GEORGE

Because we spoke about something that wasn't visible at the time. Because we mentioned something that wasn't there at the time! And do you know how I happened to notice this?

(*Pause.*)

JANNINGS

Speak.

GEORGE

When you made that motion with your hand two minutes ago—

JANNINGS

(*Interrupts him.*) Two minutes have passed since then?

GEORGE

It may also have been earlier. In any case—what was I about to say?

JANNINGS

When I made that motion with my hand . . .

GEORGE

When you made that motion with your hand, I suddenly noticed the rings on your fingers and thought to myself: ah, rings! Look at that, rings! Indeed: rings! And then I saw the rings again, and when what I thought and what I saw coincided so magically, I was so happy for a moment that I couldn't help but put the cigar box in your hand. And only then I noticed how ridiculous I had seemed to myself speaking all that time about kidneys flambé! I wasn't even myself any more, my hairs rose on end when I spoke about them. And only when I saw the rings and thought: ah, the rings!

and then cast a *second* glance at the rings, then it seemed to me that I was no longer confused.

JANNINGS
And I felt you were handing me the box voluntarily.

GEORGE
Do you understand me?

JANNINGS
From a human point of view, yes.

GEORGE
Take a look around. (*They take a look around the room.*) Car. (*They hesitate a little, continue looking around the room.*) Cattle prod. (*They hesitate, continue looking around the room.*) Bloodhounds. (*They look around the room, hesitate.*) Swollen bellies. (*Only* JANNINGS *looks around the room, hesitates.*) Trigger button.

JANNINGS
(*Quickly looks at* GEORGE.) You're right, let's talk about my rings!

GEORGE
There's nothing left to say about the rings. (JANNINGS *remains silent.*) It's meaningless.

JANNINGS
I?

GEORGE
Your rings.

JANNINGS
And?

GEORGE
(*Irritated*) "And" what?

JANNINGS
(*Irritated*) And? (*Pause. The pause becomes increasingly laden with animosity. Both smoke. When they notice that they are simultaneously drawing on their cigars, they stop and hold their breath. When one of them wants to blow out smoke, he notices that the other is just about to exhale and he hesitates; only then does he emit the smoke from his mouth.* JANNINGS *suddenly, in a very friendly manner*) And if they were *your* rings?

GEORGE
(*Suddenly looks at him in a very friendly manner.*) But they are yours! (*Pause. They hardly move. The pause becomes increasingly laden with animosity.*) But they're *your* rings? (*Suddenly* JANNINGS *pulls the rings from his fingers.* GEORGE *understands, bends forward, spreading his fingers apart.* JANNINGS *places the rings on the table.* GEORGE *slips them easily and as though routinely, almost without looking, on his fingers. He regards his hand.*) As if they were made for me! (*Pause.*) As if they had always belonged to me! (*Pause.*) They *were* made for me! (*Pause.*) And they *have* always belonged to me! (*He holds the rings up to the light so that they sparkle. He caresses them and touches each individually with his lips. He plays: points with the ringless hand at something, then points with the ringed hand at the same thing; places the ringless hand on his heart, then places the ringed hand on it; waves someone toward him with a ringless finger, then with a ringed one; threatens someone with a naked finger, then with a ringed one. He is intoxicated by the idea of ownership.*) I can't even imagine my hand without rings any more! I can't it me—I can't myself—me myself —myself me—I can't myself me—I simply can't imagine myself without rings any more! Can you imagine me without

rings? (JANNINGS *makes no reply.* GEORGE *sets out to make a speech.*) Expensive rings! Just as you, who are round, know no beginning and no end, in the same way—(*He hesitates and begins once more.*) And just as you transform the light that strikes you and are changed yourselves by the light, in the same way—(*He hesitates. Pause.*) In any cause—you elicit similes from me. Since I own you, you mean something to me. (*Pause.*) To wear rings on every finger—what does that mean? Wealth? Early death? To take care while climbing ladders? Job problems? Watch out, danger!?

(*Pause.*)

JANNINGS
I've never dreamed of rings so far.

GEORGE
Because you never owned any.

(*Pause.*)

JANNINGS
On the contrary, because I owned some. (*Pause.*) And they never elicit similes from me.

GEORGE
Because they weren't enough for you.

(*Pause.*)

JANNINGS
On the contrary, because they were enough for me.

(*Pause.*)

GEORGE
Just as . . .

JANNINGS
What do you mean, "Just—as"?

GEORGE
Bide your time! (*He begins once more.*) Just as there are born losers, born troublemakers, and born criminals . . .

JANNINGS
Who says they exist?

GEORGE
I do!

JANNINGS
That doesn't prove anything.

(*Pause.*)

GEORGE
Have you ever heard people talk about a "born loser"?

JANNINGS
Frequently.

GEORGE
And have you ever heard the expression "born troublemaker"?

JANNINGS
Indeed.

GEORGE
And the expression "born criminal"?

JANNINGS
Of course.

GEORGE
But the expression "a scurrying snake"—that you have heard quite frequently?

JANNINGS
No, never.

GEORGE
And have you ever heard of a "fiery Eskimo"?

JANNINGS
Not that I know.

GEORGE
If you don't know it, then you haven't heard of it either. But the expression "a flying ship"—that you have heard?

JANNINGS
At most in a fairy tale.

GEORGE
But scurrying snakes *exist?*

JANNINGS
Of course not.

GEORGE
But fiery Eskimos—they exist?

JANNINGS
I can't imagine it.

GEORGE
But flying ships exist?

JANNINGS
At most in a dream.

GEORGE
Not in reality?

JANNINGS
Not in reality.

(*Pause.*)

GEORGE
But born losers?

JANNINGS
Consequently, they do exist.

GEORGE
And born troublemakers?

JANNINGS
They exist.

GEORGE
And therefore there are born criminals?

JANNINGS
It's only logical.

GEORGE
As I wanted to say at the time . . .

JANNINGS
(*Interrupts him.*) "At the time"? Has it been that long already?

GEORGE

(*Hesitates; astonished*) Yes, that's odd! (*Then continues rapidly.*) Just as there are born losers, born troublemakers, and born criminals, there are (*He spreads his fingers.*) born owners. Most people as soon as they own something are not themselves any more. They lose their balance and become ridiculous. Estranged from themselves they begin to squint. Bed wetters who stand next to their bed in the morning. (The bed signifies their possession. Or perhaps their shame?) (*Brief moment of confusion, then he continues at once.*) I, on the other hand, am a born owner: only when I possess something do I become myself . . .

JANNINGS

(*Interrupts him.*) "Born owner"? I've never heard that expression.

(*Pause.*)

GEORGE

(*Suddenly*) "Life is a game"—you must have heard people say that? (JANNINGS *makes no reply, waits.*) And a game has winners and losers, right? (JANNINGS *makes no reply.*) And those who don't get anything are the losers, and those who can have everything are the winners, right? (JANNINGS *makes no reply, only bends forward, opens his mouth, but not to speak.*) And do you know the expression "born winner"?

(*Silence. Suddenly both burst out laughing and slap each other's thighs. While they are still doing so, a woman appears above left on the staircase. She is beautiful. She is wearing a long dress in which she moves as though it were carrying her. She has appeared noiselessly and has walked down a few steps. She stops in the middle of the left staircase, puts her hand on the bannister, and turns her head a little: it is* ELISABETH BERGNER. *Her hands are empty, no handbag.*)

*She observes the strange scene beneath her with lowered eyelids:* JANNINGS *and* GEORGE *are busy pulling each other's ears and patting each other's cheeks. She moves a few steps farther down and now remains standing, face forward, on the wide center staircase. With lowered eyelids she appears to observe the two below her:* JANNINGS *is just showing* GEORGE *the back of his hand;* GEORGE *replies by making a circle with his thumb and forefinger and then holding his hand in front of his face; and* JANNINGS *replies to this sign by holding both hands above his head, loosely clasping one wrist with thumb and forefinger of the other hand and letting the clasped hand circle about itself, whereupon both of them burst out laughing once again, and again start slapping each other's thighs, making exclamations such as* "Exactly!" "You guessed it!" *Then one of them slowly calms down while the other continues to slap his thighs.*

*In the meantime, two other persons have appeared on the right section of the staircase; both of them have stopped at once and observed the strange scene below: a man and a woman. One can recognize them:* ERICH VON STROHEIM *and* HENNY PORTEN. *He is impressive, wears a red dressing gown over a gray vest and pants as the only hint at a costume. She wears an evening dress with a velvet stole.*

*As they appear,* PORTEN *loudly claps her handbag shut and* VON STROHEIM *pulls up the zipper in back of her dress, then fastens his collar button:* "As I said . . ." *But it now becomes unclear how they belong together; they stand two steps apart.*

*The noise of the handbag has made one of the two downstairs gradually quiet down.* "Don't turn around!" *he says to the other.*

*The other immediately turns around and sees the three persons standing on the staircase.* "No corpse," *he says to the other.* "You can turn around: everyone is alive."

*The other turns around, then he rubs his eyes fervently.*

"Don't you believe me?" *the first one asks.*

"I just wasn't prepared for such a bright light," *he replies.* "I didn't know that it was so late already. We've lost all track of time with our talking!"

"We?" *the first one asks at once.*

"I," *answers the other.*

*Pause.*

"Yes, me too," *the first one says.*

PORTEN *is rocking back and forth on the stairway, plays with her stole; the others are rather quiet.*

PORTEN *slowly proceeds farther down the stairway, grazes* VON STROHEIM *with her stole, then exaggerates the way she steps around him.* VON STROHEIM *quickly overtakes her, stops with his back to her as if to block her path.* PORTEN *smooths down the back collar of his dressing gown, which was turned up, blows softly on his neck, and walks on. Where the two sections of the staircase join,* VON STROHEIM *stops next to* BERGNER *and bends over her neck from the back. She slowly turns around with lowered eyelids, puts her arms around his neck, leans her head against his chest.* PORTEN *has come closer, touches* BERGNER's *hip with the handbag.* BERGNER *turns her head toward her, frees herself from* VON STROHEIM, *with slow movements takes the handbag from* PORTEN *and dreamily hangs it over her own shoulder, and in the same manner offers her hand to* VON STROHEIM, *palm up. He suggests a kiss on the palm, then takes a step aside so that* POR-TEN, *who in the meantime has stepped behind him, now "takes her turn" and bends over the hand which* BERGNER *has turned over.* PORTEN *gives the incident a different interpretation by only looking at the hand over which she is bent. She straightens up, keeps the hand in hers, and guides it to* VON STROHEIM *as if she wanted to point out something on it to him.* VON STROHEIM *nods as though he saw it too. This nodding, however, gradually becomes a sign that he agrees to the following:* PORTEN *guides* BERGNER's *hand under* VON STROHEIM's *vest and moves it caressingly around,* BERGNER *suddenly withdraws the hand and lets it drop. But it is* PORTEN *who emits a brief scream. She makes a small curtsy in front of* BERGNER *and then suggests a bow in front of* VON STROHEIM. *Then she takes a step back, squints at one of the two—one doesn't know at whom—and proceeds to go down the few steps into the room.*

GEORGE *and* JANNINGS *have been the audience in the meantime. But when* PORTEN *begins to walk down, they become alert and begin to count simultaneously:* "One, two, three . . ." PORTEN *slowly descends into the room.* "Four, five, seven!" *She was just about to place her foot on the sixth step, now she hesitates as if she might fall, then runs back up the steps. She begins to walk down again.* "One, two, three, four, five, six, and seven!" *But there is also an eighth step and* PORTEN, *thinking she had reached level ground, stumbles, staggers into the room, gasps for air, and quickly runs back upstairs as if she had been repulsed. She snuggles up to* VON STROHEIM.

"Courage! Get up your courage!" *they call to her from below. They whistle the way one whistles to a dog.*

VON STROHEIM *puts his arm around her, supports her by the shoulder, proceeds to lead her slowly downstairs. Her eyes are closed.*

*The two below have started counting again.* "One, two, three, four, five, six, seven, eight, nine!" *At* "eight" VON STROHEIM *and* PORTEN *have safely arrived downstairs, but at* "nine" *they walk down one more step, one that does not exist. They bounce on the floor, go half down to their knees, stagger.* PORTEN *wants to run back but* VON STROHEIM, *who is also unsteady on his feet, leads her to a sofa. He eases her down, but while he is doing so she clutches him, feels with one hand for the sofa, and then lets herself gradually down.*

*She slowly leans back and sits there with tightly closed eyes, immobile, while* VON STROHEIM *walks step by step to the table where* JANNINGS *and* GEORGE *sit and watch. Hesitating after each movement, both hands propped up on it, he gradually sits down in the fauteuil without a footstool. He wants to lean back, stops, sits there quietly with open eyes. He blinks rapidly, with long pauses in between.*

*The audience now looks up to* BERGNER. *She stands there with lowered eyelids.* GEORGE *and* JANNINGS *tiptoe quickly to the stairs and, each holding a finger to the other's mouth, lie down parallel to the lowest step, one on his back, the other on his stomach.* BERGNER *comes down the stairs and steps over stomach and back on the floor. She is already on her way to the table. As* GEORGE *and* JANNINGS *get up and wipe the dust off each other's clothes, she has already settled in the easy chair, taken the cozy off the teapot, poured tea for herself, and, without looking up, brought the cup to her lips—as if she had done all that in one single movement.*

GEORGE *and* JANNINGS *walk back to the table, confused.*)

GEORGE

Once more: I offer you my fauteuil. (BERGNER *makes no reply.*) May I offer you my fauteuil?

BERGNER

(*As if asleep*) On the streets the insurmountable filth, the frost, the snowstorms, the immense distances . . .

JANNINGS

What did she say?

GEORGE

Nothing. She is dreaming. (*To* BERGNER, *as to someone who is talking in his sleep*) Who are you?

BERGNER

I only walked into the parlor to turn off the light and have been lost without a trace ever since.

GEORGE

Who?

BERGNER

Watch out! the candlestick is falling! (JANNINGS *and* GEORGE *turn around, but the candlestick stands motionless on the table.* BERGNER *quickly opens her eyes; screams at once*) Who are you? What do you want? Where am I? (*During these questions she has quieted down again and finished them only for form's sake. She gets up and sits down in one of the free fauteuils, but leaps up again at once.*) It's still warm! (*She tries the second fauteuil and gets up again at once.*) How dare you offer me a chair that is still warm?

JANNINGS

I?

BERGNER

No, he. (*She points at* GEORGE.)

PORTEN

(*Sitting quietly in the rear on the sofa, has opened her eyes.*) What snowstorms?

(VON STROHEIM *stops blinking his eyes and follows the conversation.*)

BERGNER

(*To* GEORGE) Why don't you answer? (*To* JANNINGS) He doesn't answer? (JANNINGS *stammers.*) Think before you speak!

(*Pause.*)

JANNINGS
(*Fluently*) Perhaps he felt you didn't expect an answer to your question.

BERGNER
Can't he answer for himself?

JANNINGS
I speak for him.

BERGNER
Are you more powerful than he is?

JANNINGS
Why? I mean, why do you ask?

BERGNER
Because you speak for him. (JANNINGS *is taken aback. He looks at* GEORGE, *who returns the glance.* JANNINGS *stammers. Pause.* BERGNER *quickly*) Does he please you? (JANNINGS *nods absentmindedly.*) Naturally, as your friend he can't help but please you.

JANNINGS
More powerful? Yes . . . Yes, why not? (*To* GEORGE) Right? I speak for you, therefore you have to listen to what I say! (GEORGE *nods playfully.*) You're not my friend! If someone has something to say here, it's me! (*Pause.* JANNINGS *and* GEORGE *begin to play.* JANNINGS *drops into the fauteuil and stretches out his feet.*) The boots! (GEORGE *quickly steps up to him, gets down on one knee, and puts on* JANNINGS's *boots.*) The tea! (GEORGE *quickly pours into a cup; hands him the cup.*) The sugar! (GEORGE *offers him the sugar bowl.* JANNINGS *takes a piece with the sugar tongs and lets it drop elegantly into the cup.*) A spoon! (GEORGE *hands him a spoon. Both grin, are close to giggling.* JANNINGS *stirs once*

*snappily with the spoon.*) The newspaper! (GEORGE *is already by the newspaper table and back.*) My glasses!

GEORGE
(*Blurts out*) But you don't wear glasses!

JANNINGS
(*Snorts.*) The mustard! The hairbrush! The . . . (*He hesitates.*)

GEORGE
(*Assists him.*) The photo album! The pincers!

JANNINGS
(*With a surgeon's gesture*) The scalpel! The scissors!

GEORGE
A permanent—and make it snappy!

JANNINGS
(*Reaching blindly behind him with gestures of an auto mechanic.*) The pliers! The monkey wrench! The soldering iron!

GEORGE
Hand over all your money—and be quick about it, if you please!

JANNINGS
The sun!

GEORGE
(*Hesitates.*) Why the sun?

JANNINGS
(*Fatigued by the game*) The sun has come up.

GEORGE
(*Confused*) Why? I mean, why do you say that?

JANNINGS
(*Snaps at him.*) Those are *my* words! (*As if exhausted*) I don't know why.

GEORGE
(*Confused, but indifferent*) Your saying so doesn't change anything. (*The last words he has spoken to himself.*)

(*In fact, the dawn light did change gradually some time ago to a normal stage light.*
*Finally one hears* VON STROHEIM.)

VON STROHEIM
Wrong! Entirely wrong! (*He gets up quickly.* BERGNER *has turned toward him; whereas she previously had turned away from the others as if disappointed.*) I'll show you how it should be done!

(*Pause. All prepare to watch.*

VON STROHEIM *takes a slow look around as if he is about to pick out someone.* GEORGE *and* JANNINGS *draw in their heads when his glance passes them. Finally* VON STROHEIM *examines* PORTEN. *Since he has his back to the audience, the fact that he is looking at her can only be gleaned from her response to him. First she leans forward, sits upright. Then she rises like a sleepwalker, walks toward* VON STROHEIM, *stops in front of him. Standing before him, she wants to take off his dressing gown, but then steps behind him and take it off from behind; while doing so, she does not seem to touch him. She walks to the tapestry door behind which the vacuum cleaner is stored, hangs the coat inside, takes out a wine-red smoking jacket;*

*back again behind* VON STROHEIM, *she spreads it out and he slips into it; again they do not touch one another.* GEORGE, *as spectator, coughs.*)

JANNINGS
Psst!

(PORTEN *pulls* VON STROHEIM's *cuffs from under his jacket sleeves. Pause.* VON STROHEIM *now describes a quarter circle with his hand, signaling* PORTEN *to stand in front of him. She obeys immediately and, in doing so, makes sure never to turn her back to him. She stops in front of him. He beckons her with his index finger to come closer. Pause.*

JANNINGS, *eagerly watching, points with a similar circular movement of his hand at the cigar box.* GEORGE, *also enthralled, has noticed the movement out of the corner of his eye and obeys blindly by handing* JANNINGS *the box from the table, still watching the two. Then he realizes what he has done and is quite startled. He looks toward* JANNINGS. *They look at one another rather startled and immediately turn back to the action.*

VON STROHEIM *pulls* PORTEN *closer to him by the stole. Playfully he steps a little to the side so that* PORTEN *is completely visible too. He grabs her with his index finger under the chin and lifts her face. Pause. He strokes the back of her head. Pause. He pats her fondly on the shoulder. Pause. He drums with two fingers on her cheek. Pause. He snaps his fingers against her teeth. Pause. He pulls her lower eyelid down with his finger. Pause. He gives her a pat on the behind so that she goes half down on her knees. Pause.* GEORGE *coughs.*)

JANNINGS
Psst!

(VON STROHEIM *turns* PORTEN *around, so that she stands with her back to him and walks back a step. Pause.* GEORGE *coughs. Still sitting,* JANNINGS *gives him a kick.* GEORGE, *standing by the table, jerks forward a little; but* PORTEN, *as if she had been kicked, tumbles across the stage toward the sofa and remains lying in front of it. In fact,* VON STROHEIM *had already lifted his knee to administer a kick. Pause. Startled, they all look at each other. Pause.*)

BERGNER
It's nice to watch when something is beginning to function smoothly. It's like watching a sale: move after move. Here the goods, there the money! Here the money, there the goods! Or like listening to two people talking: first the question, then the reply. Someone holds out his hand, the other shakes it. How are you, I'm fine! How do you like him, I think he's okay! Someone gets up, you're already leaving? Someone sighs, and you pat him. Oh, that's beautiful!

(VON STROHEIM *slowly lowers his leg, turns around slightly dazed.* PORTEN *pulls herself up on the sofa and sits down, her face half turned away.*

GEORGE *sits down bewildered in the fauteuil.* JANNINGS *looks at the boot with which he kicked him. He pinches his leg and upper arm a few times.* GEORGE, *too, fiercely pinches his arm once.* BERGNER *sighs. She walks up to* VON STROHEIM, *then stops short. He comes toward her, then stops. She takes his hand, puts it on her breast. She caresses herself with his hand until he begins to caress her.* PORTEN *suddenly gets up and runs toward the table.* GEORGE, *who from her viewpoint is sitting behind the table, stands up unintentionally.* BERGNER *and* VON STROHEIM *let go of each other and watch.*)

GEORGE
(*Asks*) What would you like? (*The words slipped out.*)

PORTEN
(*Like a customer*) Do you carry gas pistols?

GEORGE
Gas pistols? You mean "tear-gas pistols"?

PORTEN
Aren't you the salesman? (GEORGE *makes no reply*.) You were sitting behind the table and got up when I came in; you're the salesman, aren't you?

GEORGE
(*Looks at* JANNINGS, *who signifies to him to agree with her*.) The salesman? You mean I am "the salesman"? Well, why shouldn't I be the salesman? I asked you, didn't I, "What would you like?" What would you like? A weapon perhaps, for the way home after dark?

PORTEN
A tear-gas pistol!

GEORGE
(*To* JANNINGS, *who sits as if he were the boss in his fauteuil*.) Do we carry tear-gas pistols?

(JANNINGS *pulls a small riding crop out of his boot and hands it to* GEORGE, *who puts it on the table.* PORTEN *looks at it without touching it*.)

JANNINGS
(*Sits with his face turned away from her*.) This riding crop will do the trick too.

GEORGE
A riding crop like this will do the trick too.

PORTEN
I want *this* one.

JANNINGS
Is she our first customer today?

GEORGE
(*Translates.*) A customer like you should be treated like the
first customer of the day. It's yours!

PORTEN
(*Takes the crop.*) Is it a good one?

GEORGE
First-rate.

PORTEN
Can I believe you?

GEORGE
What reason would I have to trick you? (*She hands the crop
back to him, and he slashes through the air with it. One can
hear the sound. Then he slaps the crop on the table.*) Just
imagine the sound in the dark! (*He hands her the crop.*)

(PORTEN *repeats what he did, producing the same sounds.
The crop still in her hand, she pulls up her dress as far as the
hip and pulls a large note of stage money out of her garter
belt. She puts the note on the table and also places the crop
next to it.*

GEORGE, *astonished, hands the crop back to her, then takes
a few coins out of his pants pocket and puts them on the
table. While he is looking for banknotes in his other pockets,*
PORTEN *takes the coins; but when he continues to search,
she puts the coins back on the table.*

JANNINGS *gets up and flashes a few notes, which he counts
into her hand one by one. He closes her fingers one by one
over the notes; the last finger—it is the index finger—she
closes, very slowly, herself. It seems that she beckons him to*

*come to her. At the same time they look into each other's eyes. Everyone is holding his breath.*

PORTEN *pushes the bills into her bodice; then slowly withdraws her hand, making it evident that the hand is now empty; touches her upper lip with the tongue; and, gently flipping the crop back and forth, looks so long at the two salesmen that* GEORGE *shifts his weight from one leg to the other and shouts indecently loud at* VON STROHEIM: "Do you belong together?" VON STROHEIM *and* PORTEN *give each other a fleeting glance, then look away. A second glance: they look at each other as though for the first time.*)

VON STROHEIM
Can't one tell just by looking at us? (*He steps toward* PORTEN *and grabs her around the waist, and she stops flipping the crop.*)

GEORGE
I guess so, now.

PORTEN
(*To* GEORGE *and* JANNINGS) And how is it with you two? Do you belong together?

(GEORGE *and* JANNINGS *look at each other, look away. The second glance: they look at each other as though for the first time.*)

GEORGE and JANNINGS
(*Simultaneously*) Yes, he belongs to me. (*To one another,* GEORGE *softly,* JANNINGS *louder*) You belong to me—you belong to me.

GEORGE
Why?

JANNINGS
Because it has always been like that.

GEORGE
Who says that?

JANNINGS
People in general.

GEORGE
And why do you tell me that only now?

JANNINGS
There was no need to tell you until now.

GEORGE
And now it has become necessary?

JANNINGS
(*Looks at his cold cigar.*) Yes. (*He points with the cigar at the box of matches lying on the footstool.* GEORGE *bends down, then he hesitates and straightens up again.*) There, you see how necessary it was. (GEORGE, *confused, thereupon hands him the matches, and* JANNINGS, *content, lights his cigar. He drops the match.*) You've lost something there.

(GEORGE *glances briefly at the match, looks away. The second glance: he picks up the match and puts it in the ashtray.*)

VON STROHEIM
(*Applauds by way of suggestion, but one hears no clapping.*) Much better already! Much better! Of course, if I were you . . .

PORTEN
Who's stopping you?

VON STROHEIM
Yes, who's stopping me? (*He takes a deep breath and assumes a pose.* (JANNINGS *takes the coins from the table and flings them into his face.* VON STROHEIM *shakes himself and comes to his senses. He speaks to* JANNINGS *and* GEORGE *as though teaching them something.*) You're still here?

JANNINGS
(*Repeating, but twice as loud*) You're still here?

VON STROHEIM
That's it! Exactly! That's how I would have done it! (*Pause.* VON STROHEIM *gives* JANNINGS *a sign to go on speaking. He prompts him.*) What do you want here?

JANNINGS
What do you want here?

VON STROHEIM
We just want to take a look around.

JANNINGS
This isn't an amusement park!

VON STROHEIM
Why don't you let *him* speak for himself!

(JANNINGS *nods to* GEORGE *and sits down on the fauteuil, his back to the others.*)

GEORGE
This is private property. (JANNINGS *nods.*) You're not in a restaurant. You have nothing to say here. Please talk to each other only in whispers. If you must intrude here, at least take off your hats. Didn't you see the felt slippers by the entrance? Look at me: I'm talking to you. You're not at

home here, where you can put your feet on the table. What has the world come to that anybody can come in? Watch your step, man-traps and self-detonating charges have been set. Danger, rat poison. Don't touch anything. Beware of dog. Long, hard winter. Floods in spring, mud in the closets, no more cranes wake with their shrill screams in the meadows, no more June bugs buzz through the maple trees. (*Pause.*) It's terribly painful to be alive and alone at one and the same time.

(*Pause.*)

VON STROHEIM
He'll never learn it.

(*Pause.*)

GEORGE
It wasn't raining yet, but farther away one could hear it already raining . . .

(VON STROHEIM *turns away with* PORTEN *and walks around with her as if he wanted to inspect the furnishings. He wants to take out a magazine, but when he straightens up with it, it turns out that the magazine is chained to the table, like a telephone book, and he quickly puts it back. Then* PORTEN *wants to pick up the little statue covered with a paper bag, but it turns out that the statue is either screwed or glued to the chest of drawers. She pulls the bag from the statue: it is a multicolored painted dog sitting in an upright position. She touches it and it squeaks: it is made of rubber.* VON STROHEIM *joins her and pulls on one of the chest drawers. It will not open although he makes repeated attempts. Finally he tries a different drawer, which opens very easily.*)

VON STROHEIM
You see!

(*They leave the drawer open and continue their inspection tour. He takes off and drops the cover from the first picture: a seascape, not a rough sea, not a calm sea, no ships, only ocean and sky.*

*Almost simultaneously* PORTEN *has removed the cover from the second picture: a mirror without particular characteristics. She settles on the second, so far unused, sofa while* VON STROHEIM *returns from the bar with a bottle and two glasses. He sits down next to her and twists the bottle top but cannot open it. He quite casually blows into the glasses, and a cloud of dust swirls into his face. He casually puts the glasses and bottle aside. He looks at his hands, turns one palm up and down.*)

PORTEN
(*Suddenly seizes his hand.*) Watch out! (*Pause. She sees his hand.*) Oh, it's only your hand. I thought, an animal.

VON STROHEIM
Why don't you look at me?

PORTEN
I don't dare look at you closely because I'm afraid I might catch you at something! (*She looks at him.*)

(*Pause.* BERGNER *in the meantime has gone to the mirror and calmly viewed herself in it.*

GEORGE, *still standing, carefully wipes the cutlery on the table with a large red cloth he pulled out of his pocket and then places it—now and then he tries to stand it on end—on a second red cloth as if he were putting the cutlery on display. He and* JANNINGS *are spectators.*

PORTEN *has put her hand on* VON STROHEIM's *knee and is caressing her own hand with her other one.*)

VON STROHEIM

(*Moves his lips soundlessly, but every so often a word becomes audible.*) Snowplows . . . hedges . . . a dog portrait? (*At one point he presses down the intertwined fingers of both hands so that the joints crack.*)

(BERGNER *is combing herself, but with movements becoming increasingly more insecure. She does not know in which direction to comb while viewing herself in the mirror. With a small pair of scissors she wants to cut a strand of hair, holding it away from her head, but keeps missing until she finally lets go of the strand. She wants to put on makeup, pencils the eyebrows and the eyelines, puts rouge on her cheeks, powders her nose, puts on lipstick. But as she does this her movements become more and more shaky, and contradictory. She confuses the direction in which she wishes to draw the lines. She is mixed up. She wants to put the cosmetics back into the handbag but they fall to the floor. She walks away. She turns around, walks in the opposite direction, at the same time looking back over her shoulder, turns around again. She is totally confused, her face is badly made up. She walks in a direction where no one is and says:* "Help me!" *but with wrong gestures, hopping around. She bumps into things, bends forward to pick up things that physically lie behind her.*)

PORTEN

(*Calls to her.*) Open your eyes! Say something! Pull yourself together! (*But* BERGNER *does not turn her head toward her, instead to somewhere else.* PORTEN *gets up and walks up to her from behind.*) Don't be frightened.

BERGNER

(*Startled, looks up toward the stairs. She tries to point to the painting with the seascape but is unable to.*) It winked at me! It's winking at me!

(PORTEN *calms her down by caressing her and leading her around the room. Together they bend down for the coins and other things on the floor. At first* PORTEN *guides her hand, then* BERGNER *reaches for the things herself and also points at them correctly again. While doing this they talk to each other, and the longer they talk, the more sure of themselves and graceful they become.*)

PORTEN
Once when it rained I walked with an open umbrella across a wide, heavily traveled, street. When I had finally reached the other side, I caught myself closing the umbrella.

BERGNER
And once when I— Please, help me. (*She is still insecure.*)

PORTEN
(*Grabs her and wipes her face with the stole.*) Once when I bent over a bouquet of carnations while there was a great deal of noise around me, I couldn't smell anything at first.

BERGNER
Once while I wanted to put a tablecloth over . . . (*She cannot think of the word and becomes afraid again.*) Help me, please.

PORTEN
(*Speaks now very distinctly to set an example.*) Once I walked down a stairway and had such an urge to let myself fall that out of fear I began to run as soon as I had reached the bottom.

BERGNER
(*Breathes a sigh of relief.*) Once I wanted to put a tablecloth over a table, I was with my thoughts (*She neatly points to the picture.*) at the seashore and caught myself shaking the tablecloth as if wanting to wave with it.

(*They embrace, then dance around while they put the coins and cosmetics into the handbag. They talk and move more and more lightheartedly.*)

PORTEN
Why "caught"? Why not: "I saw myself," "I noticed"?

BERGNER
I saw myself! I noticed myself! I heard myself!

(*They stand facing one another.*)

PORTEN
Someone keeps looking over his shoulder while he's walking. Does he have a guilty conscience?

BERGNER
No, he simply looks over his shoulder from time to time.

PORTEN
Someone is sitting there with lowered head. Is he sad?

BERGNER
(*Assumes a modeling pose for her reply.*) No, he simply sits there with lowered head.

PORTEN
Someone is flinching. Conscience-stricken?

BERGNER
(*Answers in another modeling pose.*) No, he's simply flinching.

PORTEN
Two people sit there, don't look at each other, and are silent. Are they angry with one another?

BERGNER

(*Delivers her sentence in a new pose.*) No, they simply sit there, don't look at each other, and are silent!

PORTEN

Someone bangs on the table. To get his way?

BERGNER

(*In a different pose.*) Couldn't he for once simply bang on the table? (*They run toward each other with a little yelp of joy, embrace and separate again at once, looking at one another tensely.* BERGNER *points to* GEORGE.) He's polishing the cutlery and putting it on display on a red cloth. Does he want to sell it? (PORTEN *is standing there with arms hanging down, only shakes her head briefly.* GEORGE, *feeling as if released, now begins to polish the utensils lightheartedly.* BERGNER *points to* JANNINGS, *saying simultaneously*) He turns his back on us, sits in the most comfortable fauteuil. Does that mean he's more powerful than all of us? (PORTEN *looks into her eyes and only shakes her head briefly.* JANNINGS *stretches himself, relieved, in his fauteuil, obviously delighted to have lost his significance.* BERGNER *points with her head to* VON STROHEIM.) He's sitting alone in the corner on a big sofa. Does he want to tell us that we should sit down next to him? (PORTEN *now merely smiles as one does about something that has turned out to be a dream.* VON STROHEIM *also forgets himself, smiles amiably, and is obviously relaxing.*) And the mirror over there?

JANNINGS

(*Gets up and strolls toward the women.*) It's quite a simple mirror.

GEORGE

(*Joins in.*) Perhaps there's a flyspeck on it!

BERGNER
And why can't the drawer be pulled out of the chest?

JANNINGS
(*Hesitates just slightly.*) It's stuck.

BERGNER
And why is it stuck?

VON STROHEIM
(*Jumps off the sofa.*) Let it be stuck!

GEORGE
Yes, let it be stuck!

GEORGE and VON STROHEIM
(*Skip and dance toward each other, lifting their legs like dancing bears.*) Let it be stuck!

JANNINGS
(*Joins them.*) Let it be stuck! Let it be stuck!

GEORGE, VON STROHEIM, JANNINGS
(*The three dance around one another.*) Let it be stuck, the drawer! The drawer, oh, let it be stuck! Let it, the drawer, let it, oh, let it be stuck! (*They sing in unison.*) Oh, let the drawer be stuck, oh, oh, let the drawer be stuck! (*They stand still and sing the same words to the melody of "Whisky, Please Let Me Alone" in a canon with assigned voices, with a break in the middle, after an "Oh," whereupon they all look at one another in silence, raise their index fingers, whereupon one of them continues singing an octave lower: ". . . let the drawer be stuck!" whereupon the other two voices also join in one by one, also an octave lower, and they finish the song in harmony. They all look at one another gravely and tenderly.*) We are free? We are free! (*Pell-mell*) We only

dreamed all that! Did we only dream all that? What? I have already forgotten! And I'm just noticing how I'm forgetting! I'm standing quite still and am myself observing how I gradually forget. I'm trying to remember, but as I'm trying to remember, I notice that it sinks down lower and lower, it is as if I had swallowed something, and with each attempt to regurgitate it, it slips down lower and lower. It is sinking and you loom more and more. Where have you been, I was looking for you?! Who are you? Do I know you? (*They embrace, bend their heads toward one another, hide them, rub them together, caress each other with heads and hands. They separate and busy themselves lightheartedly with the objects: touch them, press them to their bodies, lean playfully against them, prop them up, cradle them in their arms, bring two objects into contact as for an embrace, pinch, pat, and caress them, wipe dust off them, remove hairs from them . . . While doing so, they sigh, hum, giggle, laugh, trill . . . Only once they become briefly uncertain and quiet: one of the women stands leaning against the bannister, her face turned away and her shoulders twitching. After an anxious moment, one of the men walks up to her and turns her timidly around; she is laughing quietly, and by and by they all become merry again.*

*At one time one of the men walks from an end of the stage toward the others, who are just walking toward him. He walks as if they will collide, but just when one seems to see them collide he feints with his body and steps elegantly aside. He does that across the entire stage. The other men imitate him, walk toward the women and skirt them elegantly before walking on in the same direction; the three men avoid objects the same way. They are delighted with one another, and the women laugh.*

*One of them turns a cartwheel; the other leaps merrily over an obstacle over which he could have simply stepped; the third elegantly demonstrates a gesture with his lower arm by lifting the arm and quickly bending the elbow, letting,*

*as if by magic, the sleeve slip to the elbow. He repeats this
several times, finally with the same movement giving himself
playfully a light.*

At last, quite as a matter of course, one after the other sits
down by the table, the women in the fauteuils with footstools,
VON STROHEIM *in the fauteuil without footstool,* JANNINGS *in
the easy chair,* GEORGE *in the straight chair. As in an after-
image they still hint at their previous playful acts, still repeat
what they said to one another.)* I forgot myself completely.
"I"? We! We forgot ourselves.

(*Finally they calm down. Only* BERGNER *is still playing with
her handbag and does not know where to put it.*)

VON STROHEIM
Why don't you leave it on your lap?

JANNINGS
Having something on your lap is most pleasant.

GEORGE
(*It occurred to him simultaneously.*) . . . something on your
lap is most pleasant. (*They laugh.*) In your lap you have the
most pleasant feeling for something.

PORTEN
(*It occurred to her too, but a little later.*) In your lap you
have the most pleasant feeling for something. (*They all
laugh.* BERGNER *cautiously puts the handbag on her lap, and
with little wiggling movements puts herself into a comfortable position in the fauteuil. She emits a small sound.*

*All of them try what it is like to have things on one's lap,
are satisfied, and put the things back in their places.* PORTEN
*shows her naked arm to* VON STROHEIM.) You see, I've got
goose pimples.

VON STROHEIM
Are you . . . Do you feel—(*He stops in time.*) So you have goose pimples, do you? (*He laughs.*)

(*All laugh as if it were an unpleasant memory.*)

PORTEN
Yes, I simply have goose pimples.

(*Pause.* JANNINGS *pulls something out of his upholstered seat. He holds it up and shows it to* GEORGE. *At the same time, as if unintentionally, with the index finger of the other hand he elongates one eye.* GEORGE *ignores that, bends toward what* JANNINGS *has in his hand.*)

VON STROHEIM
(*Also turns his head toward* JANNINGS. *In a playful mood*) You have something there. What is it? Nothing special, I assume? Nothing worth mentioning, I hope. There's no need to talk about it, is there?

(BERGNER *and* PORTEN *turn their heads slightly too, but look away again immediately.*)

JANNINGS
A pin. (*They all look at it, as though surprised.*)

VON STROHEIM
A pin? You don't mean "the pin"?

JANNINGS
The very one.

PORTEN
And it really exists? It isn't merely a figure of speech?

JANNINGS
Here, see for yourself.

(*He hands the pin to* GEORGE, *who hands it to* VON STRO-
HEIM *very matter-of-factly, who hands it to* PORTEN.)

PORTEN
It has all turned out to be true. Not even the ruby-red pin-
head is missing. It has all come true.

VON STROHEIM
Did you dream about it?

PORTEN
Someone mentioned it in the dream. (*She hands the pin to*
BERGNER.) When I saw the pin just now, I remembered it
again. And I had thought it was also only just another word.

GEORGE
Once someone told me about a corpse with a pinhead-sized
wound on his neck. (*Pause.*) (*To* JANNINGS) Did *you* tell
me about that?

JANNINGS
I can't remember. But when you started telling the story, it
seemed familiar to me, too.

GEORGE
No, it was a movie. (*Pause.*) It was thundering and at the
same time fog banks on the village street . . .

BERGNER
Should I drop it?

(*They all become quiet and do not move. She drops the
pin.*)

GEORGE

(*Negates the effect by speaking again too soon.*) Children with lumps of plaster on their eyes—(*He breaks off, but it is already too late. However, they only smile, leave the pin where it fell.*)

VON STROHEIM

I already told you the story about the lake?

PORTEN

No.

(*He looks at* BERGNER: *she shakes her head tenderly.*)

JANNINGS

(*Simultaneously*) No.

VON STROHEIM

Then I probably only thought of it.

PORTEN

Does it have anything to do with the pin?

VON STROHEIM

I was sitting by a lakeshore in the morning and the lake was sparkling. Suddenly I noticed: the lake is *sparkling*. It is really sparkling.

(*Pause.*)

PORTEN

Something similar happened to me one time when someone told me that his pockets were empty. "My pockets are empty!" I didn't believe him and he turned his pockets inside out. They really were empty. Incredible!

(GEORGE *takes a cigar out of the cigar box, then offers the box to* JANNINGS, *who takes out a cigar.* GEORGE *strikes a match and hands it to* JANNINGS; *he lights his cigar and blows out the match.* GEORGE *lights himself another match.*

VON STROHEIM *takes the red cloth from the table, jumps up with it, walks around with it, shakes it as if he wants to demonstrate it to them. They bend forward, inspect.* VON STROHEIM *looks around triumphantly. They nod, shake their heads surprised, laugh with delight, slap their thighs with laughter. Exclamations such as* "A red cloth, indeed!" "No doubt about it!" "Lupus in fabula," "Talk of the devil!" "Atlantis has reappeared!"

VON STROHEIM *stands in front of the others like a magician. He turns all his pockets inside out very fast—the pockets are very wide and light-colored—and strikes a pose.* PORTEN *applauds vigorously.* VON STROHEIM, *as magician, takes off his smoking jacket in a jiffy, turns it over, and already has put it back on.*)

JANNINGS
(*Enthusiastically*) So it is true! (VON STROHEIM *produces a small imitation of a rolling pin out of his pocket, which is now the magician's pocket.* JANNINGS *exclaiming so that the cigar drops out of his mouth*) Not only in jokes then! (GEORGE *hands him the cigar.* JANNINGS *wipes the ash off his knees, stops suddenly, notices what he is doing, continues cleaning in a merry ritual.*) Ash on my suit! When I tell about that, no one will believe me. (*They all laugh.* VON STROHEIM *conjures up the magician's magic cloth, a flag in colors that do not signify a particular country. He blows briskly on the flag, making it flutter.*) Indeed, it flutters! The flag flutters! (VON STROHEIM *stashes the things into his pockets, becomes an actor: he walks to the bar, takes out a bottle, fondles it, then supports himself backward with one hand on the table.* JANNINGS *calmly translates this for* GEORGE.) He is fondling the bottle and supporting himself

with his hand on the table. (VON STROHEIM *moves to the side of the table, dangles the bottle by the neck, and begins to squint.* JANNINGS *to* GEORGE) He is holding the bottle by the neck and squinting. (VON STROHEIM *puts the bottle back and moves through the room with hunched shoulders, making an unnecessarily wide curve around each object but at the same time scrutinizing each.*) He hunches his shoulders, looks at the objects, yet makes a curve around them.

VON STROHEIM
(*Returns to the table. As a teacher*) And now to the practical application: someone fondles an object or leans against it?

GEORGE
The proprietor.

VON STROHEIM
Someone moves with hunched shoulders among objects, makes a curve around them?

GEORGE
The guest.

VON STROHEIM
Someone who is squinting holds an object in his hand?

GEORGE
The thief.

JANNINGS
Someone fondles an object because it belongs to him. Because someone fondles an object, does it belong to him?

VON STROHEIM
Unless you prove the opposite.

JANNINGS
Someone with an object in his hand begins to squint. Because
he has stolen it?

VON STROHEIM
Unless he proves his innocence.

JANNINGS
Someone suddenly puckers up his mouth and nose. (*He
shows how.*) Because he's afraid and a coward?

VON STROHEIM
Unless his actions prove the opposite.

JANNINGS
But if there's nothing to do?

VON STROHEIM
What else would he be afraid of?

JANNINGS
I don't understand that.

VON STROHEIM
What you're sitting on is an easy chair, isn't it?

JANNINGS
Yes.

VON STROHEIM
Or is it perhaps a life preserver? (JANNINGS *laughs at this
extraordinary suggestion.*) It seems just as ridiculous to you
when I claim that you are sitting on a life preserver as it
would to claim that someone's mouth and nose pucker up
(*He imitates it.*) because he feels like doing something.

(*Pause.*)

JANNINGS

But an easy chair is an easy chair, and an expression (*He makes one.*) is an expression. How can the two be compared?

VON STROHEIM

I will demonstrate to you how one can. (*Pause. They all wait. Pause.* VON STROHEIM *suddenly*) What do you have in your mouth? (JANNINGS *quickly takes the cigar out of his mouth and puts it out.* VON STROHEIM *smiles.*) Why is your collar button open? (JANNINGS *nimbly closes his collar button.*) You are so serious?

(JANNINGS *laughs resoundingly. Pause. Quiet. Pause.*)

JANNINGS

(*Softly*) You have something on your nose.

VON STROHEIM

(*Is about to wipe it off, hesitates, softly*) You've understood?

(*Pause.*)

JANNINGS

(*Suddenly loud*) You're just standing there, please hand me the bottle. (VON STROHEIM *plays along, hands him the bottle.*) No, not that one, the other one! (*He points.*) No, not that one, one can't ask for anything any more. Yes, that's the one! (*But he hands the bottle back to him at once.*) Put it back in its place!

VON STROHEIM

(*Like a teacher who is playing a student*) Why?

JANNINGS

Because you took it from its place. (VON STROHEIM *nods, puts the bottle back.*) No, not there. Back in its place, I said. Over there, right.

VON STROHEIM
Why precisely there?

JANNINGS
Because that's where it stood before. (VON STROHEIM *nods.*)
Give me another bottle.

VON STROHEIM
Why?

JANNINGS
Because you gave me a bottle once before.

VON STROHEIM
That's perfect! (*He hands him the bottle.*)

JANNINGS
You're standing? (VON STROHEIM *wants to sit down on a sofa.*) Back in your place! (VON STROHEIM *sits down in his place. Playfully* JANNINGS *assigns the following roles: he hits the bottle neck with a teaspoon:* GEORGE *gets up.* JANNINGS *without looking at him*) Cartwheels! (GEORGE *stands there.*)

VON STROHEIM
(*Prompts him.*) Why?

GEORGE
Why?

JANNINGS
Because you did a cartwheel before! (*Pause.* GEORGE *turns a cartwheel.* JANNINGS *hands him the magazine.* GEORGE *does not yet understand this language; he doesn't know what to do with the magazine, glances into it.*) Hand it on.

GEORGE
Why?

JANNINGS

Didn't you also hand on the pin before? (*Pause.* GEORGE *hands the magazine to* VON STROHEIM; *he gives it back to* GEORGE *as if the pages were mixed up.* GEORGE *understands: he arranges the pages and hands the magazine back to* VON STROHEIM, *who puts it on the table.* JANNINGS *pulls the second red cloth from under the cutlery on the table and lets it drop. He points to it with the spoon. Pause.*) Well?

GEORGE

Why?

JANNINGS

Didn't you just do a cartwheel?

GEORGE

But how can you compare the two?

JANNINGS

For whom, then, did you do the cartwheel?

GEORGE

For you—(*He hesitates.*)

JANNINGS

"Of course" you wanted to say, right?

GEORGE

For you, of course.

JANNINGS

If you can do a cartwheel for me, you can also pick up a cloth for me.

(*Pause.*)

GEORGE

(*Wants to bend down for the cloth, hesitates.*) But what if I don't want to?

JANNINGS

Now it's too late for that. All the time you did as I asked you to and never said anything. You were content until now or you would have said something. So why should you be dissatisfied now? You didn't contradict me at any time. Why should you be allowed to contradict me now? No, what you utter now doesn't count any more. Do as I say! (*Pause.* GEORGE *picks up the cloth, wants to hand it to* JANNINGS, *who doesn't even bother to extend his hand, hesitates, lets it drop again "as if his hand has fallen asleep." Pause.* JANNINGS *in a sensible tone of voice*) Look at the others. (*He turns his head to* VON STROHEIM, *then to* PORTEN. VON STROHEIM *goes at once with the guitar—which he takes out of the bag while walking—up to* BERGNER, *sits down behind her and quaintly strikes two soft chords.* PORTEN *sits down on* JANNINGS's *knees and makes herself comfortable.*) If *they* do as they're told—why don't you too?

(*Pause.*)

GEORGE

But why do they do it?

JANNINGS

First obey. Then we can talk about it. (*Pause.* GEORGE *hands him the cloth, which* JANNINGS *places picturesquely around* PORTEN's *shoulders, and ties under her chin. To her*) Well? (*She kisses him without moving her head.*) Now ask!

GEORGE

Why do they do that? Why do they listen to you?

(VON STROHEIM *strikes another quaint chord.*)

JANNINGS

Because it is natural to them. They did it once without my saying anything while they were half asleep, or because it just happened like that. Then I said it and they did it again. Then they asked me: "May I do that for you?" and I said: "You shall!" And from then on they did it without my having to say anything. It had become the custom. I could point my *foot* at something and they would jump and get it. Nothing but laws of nature. People began to socialize with one another and it became the rule.

BERGNER

(*On cue, as though talking in her sleep*) How are you; I'm fine, thanks. (*She sighs.*)

JANNINGS

An order resulted; and for people to continue to socialize with one another, this order was made explicit: it was formulated. And once it had been formulated, people had to stick to it because, after all, they had formulated it. That's natural, isn't it? Say something! No, don't say anything, *I* am speaking now. Don't touch that, it's mine! (*He pushes a candlestick away.*) Don't dare to stare at it, it's my property! What was I talking about? Help me! No, don't say anything. About the laws of nature. (*He takes an ashtray into his hand, then lets it drop.*) Just as this ashtray obeys the law of gravity, so you obey me. Well? (*He points with his foot;* GEORGE *puts the ashtray back on the table.*) You see? Do you believe me now? No, don't answer, I'll answer for you. Yes, that business with the ashtray and the force of gravity is true enough, I can imagine your answer to be. Do you know what the difference is between you and me? (GEORGE *laughs as though before a joke.*) No, no joke: I *can* imagine you sometimes, you *must* imagine me always. Why aren't you laughing? By the way, this reminds me of a real joke: what's the man's name who invented the chair? Well? Nothing? I'll help you. What's the man's name who invented the Zeppelin? (*Pause. He laughs invitingly.*) You're not laughing. O.K.! But I'll make a note of it. Where was I? Hadn't I asked you to remind me what else I wanted to talk about? Didn't I see you nod? Then I only imagined that I saw you nod. Once I thought of a conversation I had with someone, and I remembered distinctly how he'd smiled when he answered me, and then it occurred to me that I had been talking to him on the telephone! The laws of nature! The trains! The ocean! He stood where you're standing now! (GEORGE, *startled, steps aside;* JANNINGS *bursts out laughing, again drops the ashtray.*) I'd like to pick it up for you, but I have to stick to what I said (*To* PORTEN), don't I? (*She nods.*) I can't say something and then do the opposite of what I've said. Inconceivable! That would be a topsy-turvy world. Do you understand that? (PORTEN *tries to reach backward for the ashtray.*) Stop, that's *his* job! (GEORGE *puts the ashtray on the table,* VON STROHEIM *touches the guitar almost accidentally: a gentle chord.*) So you understand. Just as the trains must obey a schedule so that there is no disorder, so you must obey me. That business with the trains and their schedule is probably true, you say? I dare you to tell me that! Keep quiet? Answer! (GEORGE *wants to speak.*) Forget it! Like a maggot that crawls across one's palm—no, that belongs somewhere else. The ocean! What are you thinking of just now? You can't say it? Then you're not thinking of anything. I once lived for some time by the ocean, and since I lived there, in what categories would you guess I began to think? In the categories of low and high tide! And that's how it is generally: (*As though to the audience*) the manner in which one thinks is determined by the laws of nature! (*Again to* GEORGE) For example, since I've started taking walks through the woods, I always think at the sight of the weak and the strong in terms of the laws of nature. And since I learned to read menus—(*He pushes* PORTEN *from his knees and she goes quickly to the sofa, cuddles up on it, and he looks toward her.*)—I think about women, whether I want to or not, in the categories of hors d'oeuvre and main dish. (*She looks at him, but one rather feels the look than actually sees it.*) She doesn't want it differently—ask her yourself. She'll show you how. (*He snaps his fingers at her and she responds.*)

BERGNER

(*As though she had learned a few questions by heart*) Do I talk too much for you? Are my knees too bony? Am I too heavy for you? Is my nose too big? Am I too sensible for you? Do you find me too loud? Are my breasts too small? Do you think I'm too fat? Am I too fast for you? Am I too skinny for you? Was I good?

JANNINGS

You see, she herself uses the categories in which one thinks of her. (*To* PORTEN) Hey! (*She comes back and settles on his knees.*) When *I* used to be called, to begin with I only said "yes!" After all, it was possible that they only wanted to know whether I was still there. Where were we? (GEORGE *puts his hand to the back of his head, lowers the hand again.*) Stop! Repeat that gesture! (GEORGE *repeats it.*) It reminds me of something. More slowly! (GEORGE *repeats the gesture.*) The hat! Do you know the song "Me Hat, It Has Three Corners"? It's a folk song. (*He recites it seriously.*)

> Me hat, it has three corners
> Three corners has me hat
> And if it hadn't three corners
> It wouldn't be me hat.

Ever since I've known that song I am incapable of imagining a hat with it. A three-cornered hat: an impossible idea! A hat: an impossible, a forbidden idea! Once I ordered (or permitted?) a cake to be cut. "Where?" I was asked. Ever since then I've been unable to imagine a cake. You try drawing a circle in your mind but don't know where to begin. Finally there's a noise in the brain as if a boiling egg were popping. Quiet! Shut up! I can imagine what you want to say! The circle! I become dizzy when I'm supposed to imagine it! And when I become dizzy, I become furious. For example, someone asks me what time it is. Can you imagine that there's someone who has no watch? I certainly can't. Dizziness and anger! Or: a person looks "desperate," starts all sorts of jobs but stops them all again at once. Can you imagine anyone still being seriously desperate? Dizziness! Dizziness and anger! Or someone is ashamed? Dizziness and anger, dizziness and anger! Then the contrary: someone is ashamed for someone else? I for you? At once! You cannot imagine that I'm ashamed for you? (*He pushes the cigar box off the table so that all the cigars fall out, puts* PORTEN *in her fauteuil, stands in front of* GEORGE, *and claps his hands before* GEORGE's *face, pretending to slap him, and sits down again.*) Like chocolate and soap—yes, like chocolate that lies next to a piece of soap. I, at any event, have never felt ashamed—except for that time when I compared two feelings I had for someone to chocolate and soap. And then once more. (*Pause.*) And then the story about the maggot on the palm of the hand. (*Pause.*) And then once when I was asked: "Who is that?" and answered: "That one? Yes, she's very touching, isn't she?" (*Pause.*) Yes, and then one more time. (*He laughs shamefully, remembering.*) And then once when I said: "Present company excepted, naturally!" And another time when I heard someone say, "She's ugly!" and replied: "But she has pretty eyes." (*Pause.*) And then just the one more time when I put the matchbook on the counter and the salesman asked me: "Is that *you?*" (*Pause; puzzled*) Actually, I've been ashamed quite frequently. (*Pause, to* VON STROHEIM) Should I make *him* feel ashamed?

VON STROHEIM
(*Strikes the body of the guitar and spreads his fingers.*) Just so you aren't put to shame by him!

JANNINGS
(*Turns to* GEORGE.) Look over here! (*Successively he takes
several objects from the table or out of his pocket and shows
them to* GEORGE. GEORGE *looks helplessly at each of them.
Finally* JANNINGS *shows him some paper money, waves it,
and* GEORGE *quickly tries to grab it.* JANNINGS *laughs.*) This
language he understands! This language he understands! (*He
laughs again. Pause. They both bow their heads.* JANNINGS
*scratches himself once vigorously. Suddenly he points angrily
at the cigars.*) What's that?

GEORGE
Cigars.

JANNINGS
And what's that supposed to mean? Pick them up! (GEORGE
*bends down.* JANNINGS *giggles.*) Can you still imagine doing
anything but what I tell you to? (GEORGE *tries to imagine it.
Finally he also starts giggling, but stops again and tries to
think once more.*) Imagine you're sitting in my place.
(GEORGE *looks up at him. He begins to giggle.* JANNINGS
*giggles too, but differently; he looks around himself.*
PORTEN *is also giggling.* VON STROHEIM *is smiling.* BERGNER *is
absentminded.* GEORGE *collects the cigars and puts them
carefully back in the box.* JANNINGS, *while watching him, tells
a story.*) Once—(*To* PORTEN) Why are you grinning?

PORTEN
I'm not grinning, I'm smiling.

JANNINGS
Stop fidgeting!

PORTEN
I'm not fidgeting, I'm making myself comfortable.

JANNINGS
Shut your trap!

PORTEN
I don't have a trap.

JANNINGS
(*Has already turned back to his story.*) . . . I had a bad day,
you know how that is. (GEORGE *nods.*) I burned my tongue
on the coffee; as I was tying my shoelaces, I suddenly had
two pieces in my hand, you know what that's like. (GEORGE
*nods.*) Just as suddenly—why "just as suddenly"? What's the
difference! In any case, as I'm writing down what I plan to
do, the tip of the pencil breaks off. I look for another pencil—
no, not what you're thinking: the pencil does write; however, all at once I noticed that overnight I've begun to write
one letter differently from the way I used to, with a curlicue
where I never before made a curlicue during my entire life!
You know what that's like. (GEORGE *nods, but only after*
JANNINGS *has looked at him.*) To top it all, I suddenly see
before me a woman trampling furiously on eggshells. I tear
her away by the hair, you know what that's like. But it
turns out that she is purposely breaking up the shells for the
birds. Dazed, I walked on and notice another madman. He's
running back and forth on a piece of land, and a crowd has
already formed around him. Then it turns out that he isn't
mad at all but the owner of the land trying to keep people
from trespassing. Even more dazed, I walk on and am
thinking about a goose I'm in the process of carving up, very
fastidiously, you know what I'm like, not to get any grease
stains on my suit, when someone grabs me by the arm from
behind. Despite, or just *because* of, my dazed state—(*He
smirks.*) Whenever I say *despite,* I also must say, *just because
of*—I swiveled around and gave this someone a box on the
ear. My hand slipped; you know what that's like: I thought
someone with greasy fingers had grabbed me. Suddenly—

yes, again *suddenly,* that day passed in leaps and bounds—I stood before a dog that squatted with quivering behind at the curb—*quivering:* I've never used that word before!—and wanted to do his business, you know what that's like. I, no lazybones myself—(*To* GEORGE, *who hesitates*) Don't let me stop you from your work—gave him a kick . . .

PORTEN
Don't go on, please! I don't want to have to dream about it.

GEORGE
Once my mind was on a child and a hot iron, and when I suddenly saw someone reaching for the door handle, I shouted at him: *Don't touch!*

JANNINGS
You can talk and stack cigars *evenly* at one and the same time? (GEORGE *continues to work in silence,* JANNINGS *goes on talking.*) . . . and went home. Luckily the sun set very rapidly, as it always does in the tropics—that's how it is described in all narratives, isn't it?—and as I slowly open the door, there is a soft rustling behind it. (*Slowly* and *softly* generally belong together.) I immediately fired through the panel—and I myself had spread the papers on the floor to frighten the burglars when they'd open the door. A bad day! Later in my rocking chair I dozed off. Suddenly I awake and see the dog running past me. A quick slap with the riding crop—you know what that's like? (GEORGE *nods.*) But it was my own feet: when I jerked awake, I took my black socks for the dog. (*Pause.*) You have nothing to say?

GEORGE
I feel no need to say anything.

JANNINGS
It's enough that I feel the need to hear something from you.

GEORGE
But what if I feel the need to remain silent?

JANNINGS
Then you must say to yourself that in regard to your needs, what matters for you is to learn to need to do what you must do in any case. (*Pause.*) Say something!

(*Pause.*)

GEORGE
But what did you want to prove with the story? You didn't tell the story just to tell a story?

JANNINGS
I told it so you would know what it is like when a whole day passes and one feels out of sorts.

GEORGE
Out of sorts with what?

JANNINGS
With one's work.

GEORGE
You weren't working at the time?

JANNINGS
I was working, but I felt out of sorts with my work.

GEORGE
And what is it like if one feels out of sorts with one's work while one is working?

JANNINGS
I told you: a swift sunset, a rustling behind the door, strange dogs in the room.

GEORGE
And what is it like if one does not feel out of sorts with one's work while one is working?

JANNINGS
It becomes a game.

GEORGE
And how do you manage not to feel out of sorts while you work?

JANNINGS
One must imagine that it's a game.

GEORGE
And who determines the rules of the game?

JANNINGS
The one who plays it: the one who works.

GEORGE
Is it like that or does one have to imagine it?

JANNINGS
If you're not out of sorts, it's like that.

GEORGE
But if I feel out of sorts, then I first have to imagine it?

JANNINGS
If you feel out of sorts, you cannot imagine it. Instead: a swift sunset, a rustling behind the door . . .

GEORGE
But I feel out of sorts.

JANNINGS

I'll show you. (*He gets up and puts a cigar in the box with playful little movements, a finger dance. Then he sits down.*) For me work is a game.

GEORGE

Well, it isn't *your* work. But it is your *thing*. And it's up to you to tell me how *my* work with *your* thing can be called a game. I who feel out of sorts—you're right—cannot imagine it.

(*Pause.*)

JANNINGS

You must regard work like a bet: whoever is faster, more elegant, more thorough—then there are winners and losers.

GEORGE

But with whom am I supposed to bet when I'm by myself?

JANNINGS

With yourself.

GEORGE

Whether I'm faster than myself?

JANNINGS

No smart talk! You can't allow yourself to be ironical until you've finished your work . . . Don't you have two hands?

GEORGE

Obviously.

JANNINGS

Which hand is more nimble?

GEORGE

The right one, I suppose.

JANNINGS

Then make a bet with yourself and give it a try. (*Pause.* GEORGE *starts putting cigars back in the box first with his left, then with his right hand. He becomes increasingly faster, gets into a frenzy. He has finished and puts the box on the table.*) Which hand won?

GEORGE

(*Remains silent. Speaks suddenly.*) Let's bet on something else.

JANNINGS

Fine, let's make a bet.

GEORGE

(*Points to* PORTEN.) You turn her over your knee and spank her.

JANNINGS

And what's the bet?

GEORGE

First turn her over your knee. (JANNINGS *puts* PORTEN *over his knee.*) You hit her with the riding crop as fast as you can for one minute. While doing so you keep your mouth shut. If you open it, you've lost.

JANNINGS

It's a bet. (*Pause. He starts beating her vigorously, but already after a few slaps his lips part. Startled, he lets go of her and sits down, pinches his lips tight. He wipes his forehead.* GEORGE *also sits down. Pause.* VON STROHEIM *touches the guitar as if by chance. A very gentle sound. He laughs.* JANNINGS *opens his mouth as if to roar and wants to hit the table. He shuts his mouth again instantly and lets his fist sink, opens his fingers.*) I believe—(*He breaks off; he wants to reach for something but stops in midair and lets his hand drop.*)

GEORGE
(*To* PORTEN) You'd better imagine it all once more right now; then you won't need to dream of it later on—

PORTEN
(*Smiles.*) Of water and of madness, of . . .

VON STROHEIM
(*At the other end, wanted to say something at the same time.*) I was so very . . .

(*They both break off. Pause.*)

PORTEN
(*Turns again to* GEORGE.) Of water and of madness, of ships of fools on great rivers where . . .

VON STROHEIM
(*Again at the same time, to* BERGNER) I was so very much afraid. I was so very much afraid for . . .

(*Pause.*)

JANNINGS
(*Points to* VON STROHEIM *while looking at* PORTEN.) It's his turn.

(*Pause.*)

VON STROHEIM
(*As in a game, to* BERGNER) I was so very much afraid for you that I suddenly burst out laughing. You were sitting there and didn't move. Only your jugular vein throbbed.

BERGNER

I haven't been listening. (*He bends over her, but so that she has to see his face upside down. She opens her eyes, a small cry of horror; he turns his head so that she sees his face normally again, and she calms down instantly and looks at the guitar.*) Is that for me? (VON STROHEIM *hesitates, hands it to her.*) And what do I have to do for that? (*She turns the guitar around as if it were a present, then hands it back.* VON STROHEIM *puts the guitar on the table. He strokes* BERGNER's *neck with his finger. Pause.* BERGNER *slaps his hand.*) Don't touch me!

JANNINGS

(*Prompts.*) Why?

VON STROHEIM

Why don't you want to be touched? You used to let people touch you.

BERGNER

Don't look at me!

VON STROHEIM

A little while ago you looked at me tenderly.

BERGNER

Does that mean that I should "look at you tenderly" now, too? (VON STROHEIM *posts himself in front of her. She looks away.*) Every time you men begin to speak, it is as if a beggar is trying to talk to me.

VON STROHEIM

All of us men?

BERGNER

Yes, you too.

VON STROHEIM
Give me your hand.

BERGNER
Why? (*He takes her hand.*) Are you a palm reader? (VON STROHEIM *strokes her hair.*) I know that my hair is a mess.

VON STROHEIM
You are beautiful.

BERGNER
Have you seen my handbag anywhere?

VON STROHEIM
(*Puts a necklace around her neck.*) What do I get for that?

BERGNER
Why do you have to spoil my necklace for me?

VON STROHEIM
What must I do to make you stop despising me? Is it the way I move that you dislike? Is it my hairline? Is it the way I hold my head that makes you look away? Do the hairs on my hands disgust you? Do you find it exaggerated the way I move my arms up and down when I walk? Do I talk too much? (PORTEN, *watching from some distance away, laughs. Pause.* VON STROHEIM *as on the telephone*) Are you still there? (BERGNER *looks at him.*) Where were you? Why don't you say something? Do say something! Come back! You were so beautiful, it was painful to look at you; so beautiful that I was suddenly very much afraid for you. You were so painfully beautiful that you left me behind—me, who was suddenly so alive—left me behind—terribly *alone*. You said nothing, and I talked to you as one talks to those who have just died: Why don't you say something? Do say something! Can you imagine it?

(*Pause.*)

BERGNER

Not any more. For a moment—(*Pause.*) No. It's over.

VON STROHEIM

Don't stop talking, I am afraid to break in when you stop talking. Right now my tenderness for you is so vehement that I want to hit you.

(*Pause. He hits her. She stands up. He stares at her. She lets him stare at her.*

*Abandoning the long rigidity, she moves slowly and walks up and down in front of him. She interrupts her smooth movements now and then to turn jerkily, leans her hand on the hip, stretches herself loosely, lets her arms drop, while moving like this, grazes a number of objects, supports herself everywhere, once swings around to* VON STROHEIM, *stops in front of him, takes off her necklace. She is standing there as if she has just come through a door and has leaned against it. She strokes him with the necklace and lets it drop into his pocket.*)

BERGNER

(*Looks at him.*) Don't move! (*He wants to touch her, she stands still, smiling; he hesitates briefly, now touches her neck and wants to pull her toward him; but he is a moment too late, her neck resists him, she shakes off his hand and steps back.*) Why don't you look at me as if you didn't care?

VON STROHEIM

For that I would have to imagine that you were mine.

BERGNER

Then imagine it.

VON STROHEIM

Where should I begin?